God is not 'Green'
A Re-examination of Eco-theology

God is not 'Green'
A Re-examination of Eco-theology

Adrian Michael Hough

First published in 1997

Gracewing
Fowler Wright Books
2 Southern Ave, Leominster
Herefordshire HR6 0QF

© Adrian Hough 1997

The right of Adrian Hough to be identified as the author of this work has been asserted in accordance with the Copyright, Designs and Patents Act 1988.

ISBN 0 85244 307 2

Typesetting by
Action Typesetting Ltd, Gloucester, GL1 1SP

Printed by Cromwell Press
Broughton Gifford, Wiltshire, SN12 8PH

Contents

Preface

Before I began my training for the ordained ministry, I worked as a research chemist. In my work, I tried to account for and to understand both the chemistry of the natural atmosphere and the changes which are caused by atmospheric pollution. It was therefore natural for me to want to apply theological thinking and analysis to the situations which I was used to examining as a scientist, namely the natural order of the world both without and within the influences of human activity. In particular I wanted to examine the ways in which Christian doctrine and practice could provide an adequate response to the environmental problems now facing the Earth.

This issue increased in importance for me in Holy Week 1990 during my first year at theological college. I was closely involved in planning the worship for the college, but suddenly found myself in demand for television, radio and newspaper interviews following the publication of a scientific paper which I had written shortly before beginning my theological training. In one of these interviews, the interviewer made something of my change in vocation and concluded the interview by asking me if I thought that God was green. Here at last is my answer to that question.

There can be no doubt that the question of whether traditional Christian doctrine can provide an adequate response to the present ecological concerns is an important issue to address. Much of the current theological writing in this area would appear to answer this question in the negative and to advocate radical changes to the way in which we understand both God and the Christian tradition. Such conclusions should not be allowed to go unchallenged.

This book is not a systematic account of the whole of theology in an environmental context, nor does it claim to address every issue or provide solutions to every problem. A book of this length can only be an introduction to or an overview of the subject. Indeed, it is quite possible that the present work raises more questions than it answers, particularly with regard to the implications of such thinking for ecclesiology and worship. However, this asking of questions is both a part of theology and also a part of the process of showing that traditional Christian doctrine and practice can address the present environmental issues in the world – a view which is not often heard. Both as Christians and as a Church we need to come to a greater understanding of our doctrines and practices, an understanding which needs to be present in the local Church as well as in places where theology is taught. Above all, we need to be prepared and able to explain our understanding to a world which is looking for answers to the serious problems which it faces at the present time.

I am grateful to a number of people who have assisted my thinking on the issues which I discuss in the following pages. Several members of the staff at Ripon College Cuddesdon made favourable comments on essays which I used to try out some of my ideas without them being aware of my intentions. Judith Bersweden, Hazel Bradley, Iain Luke and Richard Reade all encouraged me to start writing, whilst Bill Richards has since provided me with the time which I needed in order to write. John Guise read through the whole of the initial draft. My wife Kathryn allowed me to purchase a Personal Computer together with the upgrades and software which I have added over the years. The staff at Gracewing/Fowler Wright have helped me to turn my first attempts at writing a book into something which we believe makes sense and Paul Haffner made a number of important suggestions for improving the final manuscript.

Finally, whilst I was engaged in writing the manuscript, I had the pleasure of helping a group of young people as they prepared for Confirmation. In their various ways, what Helen, Katharine, Toby, Vicky, Venessa, Hayley and Amanda have confirmed for me, is that provided we attempt to answer the questions which people are really asking then traditional Christian Doctrine does stand some chance of making sense in the modern world.

Adrian Hough
Broadwas-on-Teme

Chapter 1

Theology and Ecology

1.1 Introduction

We live in an age which is marked by an increasing concern for the environment and for the way in which it is being damaged by the human race. There is scarcely a day that passes without our hearing of another threat to the natural world. This widespread concern has resulted in the appearance of many scientific publications and research reports which address the damage which is being caused and how this damage might be prevented. However, it is not only the scientific community which has responded in this manner. There has also been a wide range of theological publications concerned with environmental issues. In some of these, serious attempts have been made to answer the theological questions which are raised by the current ecological concern.[1]

These theological questions usually begin with our understanding of the Christian doctrine of creation. If we acknowledge the existence of God, of a God who was or is involved with creation in some way, then how are we to understand that God when faced by ecological and environmental problems in that same creation? How can Christian theology relate to the issues involved in such ecological damage and what can it say about them, which both recognises their scientific complexity and is also relevant to the modern Church? Moreover, is it possible for theologians to respond in this way, whilst both remaining true to the theological tradition which has been established over the past two millennia and also accepting the insights of modern biblical and theological scholarship?

These are major and very serious questions which the Christian Church needs to address if it is to be credible and relevant to the modern world and to the problems which it now faces. They are also important questions because much of this theological thinking on ecological issues results in conclusions which differ markedly from traditional Christian doctrine.

Whenever the Church develops new ideas in response to new situations, it always needs to question whether these ideas are truly Christian or whether the Gospel is being diluted and side-tracked by concepts which, although interesting, are contrary to Christian teaching. In many cases these so-called developments amount merely to a rediscovery of ideas already known to theology and which have often been rejected as heretical. Such developments can actually serve to limit theology and to stifle its development.

There is an interesting parallel to this situation which occurred in the life of the people of Israel when they reached the end of their Exodus from Egypt under the guidance of Moses. The people of Israel had to enter Canaan and adopt the agricultural practices which they found there, as these were necessary if they were to be successful in cultivating the land. In doing this they had to take care that they did not also adopt the indigenous religious customs of the land and worship the local fertility gods. We know that they failed in their attempt and that they succumbed to such nature worship. The criticism of this failure is found in a number of Old Testament writings, in particular those books which are attributed to the Deuteronomaic schools of writing, such as Deuteronomy and parts of Kings and Jeremiah.

In our current context there is one phrase found in these writings which is particularly evocative. In the Revised Standard Version of the Bible this is translated as 'Under every green tree', usually with reference to the worship of false gods and idols which occurred near prominent trees on hill-tops. Reference to such worship often uses the language of prostitution, as the people 'give' themselves to other gods. Worship of such idols is condemned in passages such as: Deuteronomy Ch.12 v2; II Kings Ch.16 v4 and Ch.17 v10; Isaiah Ch.57 v5; Jeremiah Ch.2 v20, Ch.3 v6-10 and Ch.3 v13; Ezekiel Ch.6 v13 and Hosea Ch.4 vv12-13. In each of these passages, reference is made to Judah or Israel prostituting themselves in following the fertility gods and adopting religious practices which were alien to their own cult. In attempting to meet the theological needs of an environmentally conscious or 'green' age, the Christian Church needs to ensure that it does not face the same accusations. It should not and need not abandon its traditional doctrines and beliefs and go in search of 'green ideologies' in an attempt to become relevant to the passing age.

This does not mean that the Christian faith cannot use the natural world, either in its worship or in proclaiming its message. If this world was created by God and if it is indwelt by His Holy Spirit, then there is every reason why we should use such symbols. Celtic spirituality provides a good example of this technique. Celtic Christianity appropriated the symbols of natural or pagan religion and used them for its own purposes and within its own doctrines. It used an imagery which was relevant to those to whom it spoke, but it used it to proclaim its own message and not that which it found along with the symbols. This was a risky business and sometimes led to difficulties, but it was generally successful in converting pagan peoples to Christianity.

The Christian Church of today needs to take this message to its heart. We need to understand what we are doing and what Christian doctrine is actually saying, rather than attempting to incorporate other ideas or invent new theologies every time we encounter a new situation. The process of 'doing theology' should be the application of doctrine and biblical materials in order to respond to the situations and questions of the age. It should not be about inventing new ideas and ideologies because they happen to suit us at the time. This does not mean that modern biblical scholarship and doctrinal developments are to be ignored, they are rather to be used to the full, but they are to be used within the context of the whole body of Christian thought. It is this whole body which should be used to 'do theology' and respond to the questions of the present day.

In 1990 the radio interviewer asked me if God is green. My answer is, that the God who created the world and who continues to care for that world is 'green', if by this we mean that He is in tune with and works for all that is natural and good and cares for the environment. On the other hand, God is not 'green', if by this we imply that he is the product of the 'Green Movement' and that traditional Christian understanding is so seriously flawed that we have to recreate our image and understanding of God.

I believe that the human race is doing immense damage to the world which it inhabits and that Christianity may have played its part in the development of this problem. At the same time, I do not believe that this Christian involvement is due to some fundamental flaw in the Christian faith, but rather to the way in which Christian doctrine has been misunderstood and abused over the years. However, before we can address these issues, it is important that we also understand the nature of the problem which the world is facing. If we do not understand the problem then neither can we hope to answer the questions which arise from it.

1.2 The Polluted Environment

Although the prospect of nuclear conflict and the human exploitation of the earth's resources have been public considerations since the 1940s, it was only in the mid 1980s that a more general public awareness of ecological problems emerged. At this time both politicians and theologians started to consider the implications of these issues in detail. Amongst the most pressing topics for discussion were the clearance of tropical rain forests, acid-rain, global warming and the disposal of nuclear waste and other toxic products. During this same period there was also a marked increase in the concern shown by the scientific community for the changes which the human race is causing in the global atmosphere. Following the thaw in relations between East and West, it is likely that such atmospheric pollution now poses the greatest threat to the continuation of life on Earth as we know it.

Human understanding of the physical and chemical processes which occur in the atmosphere has improved greatly during the above period, but little progress has been made in solving most of the problems associated with atmospheric pollution. Indeed, the various types of pollution and the issues which are involved with their production and control are often misunderstood and misrepresented by those with no specialist knowledge of the subject and this can lead to erroneous advice and opinion. It would therefore seem prudent to examine these issues from a scientific perspective before attempting a theological approach to these complicated subjects.

Although pollution of land, rivers and seas is undoubtedly important, it is atmospheric pollution which probably poses the greatest long-term threat to the environment. Such pollution occurs in many forms and over a wide range of spatial scales. These range from effects which are largely local in scale, such as the emission of lead from motor-vehicle exhausts in vehicles which use leaded petrol, through regional-scale problems such as acid deposition[2] and the production of photochemical oxidants[3], to global problems such as damage to the ozone layer[4] and the global perturbation of the troposphere (approximately the bottom ten kilometres of the atmosphere). This final category manifests itself in the possibilities of global warming (the so-called 'greenhouse effect')[5] and a global increase in the abundance and turnover of photochemical oxidants.[6]

Acid deposition occurs both in rain and at other times (dry deposition) when acidic products formed from the emissions of fossil-fuel fired power stations and motor-vehicles are deposited on the earth's surface. Most of this deposition occurs within about a thousand miles of where the emissions occur and is complete within a few days.

Photochemical oxidants are produced on both a similar time-scale and in similar areas to acid deposition and result from the action of strong sunlight on vehicle exhaust emissions and the hydrocarbons released by industry – largely industrial solvents. The most usual photochemical oxidant is ozone. This gas is poisonous, can cause asthma and in the workplace is subject to limitations on exposure.

Damage to the ozone layer occurs due to the emission of halocarbons, mainly chlorofluorocarbons, often referred to as CFCs. The ozone layer is situated some twenty kilometres or more above the surface of the earth and shields life from ultraviolet radiation emitted by the Sun. Whereas at ground-level, ozone is dangerous, at higher altitudes it is vital if life on

Earth is to survive. Halocarbons can remain in the atmosphere for many years, so that the threat from this form of pollution continues for between fifty and two-hundred years after the emission of the halocarbons has ceased, depending on the specific chemicals which are involved.

The global perturbation of the troposphere is caused by the emission of a wide-range of chemical species from sources all over the world. Most of these chemicals are emitted naturally, but the balance and composition of the atmosphere is being altered by the extra emissions which occur due to the growth in human activities associated with industry, transport, food-production and the decomposition of domestic waste.

However, atmospheric pollution does not only affect air-quality. The dry deposition of gases and aerosol particles (microscopic particles formed by chemical reactions in the atmosphere) can result in the acidification of the underlying surface whether this consists of buildings, vegetation, soil or water. Similarly, precipitation will incorporate any water-soluble gases, such as nitric and sulphuric acids, and deposit them on the underlying surface which again results in acidification. Although nitric acid can have a beneficial effect on the fertility of soils which are poor in nitrogen, the deposition of these compounds can disturb the complex chemical balance in the soil and surface waters. This can reduce crop yields, damage trees and lower fish stocks.

Water in rivers and streams can also be contaminated by nitrates and pesticides which originate in farming and horticulture,[7] as well as by sewage and accidental chemical spillage by industry. These pollutants ultimately reach the marine environment where they are joined by, for example, further sewage and crude oil.

The waste products of the nuclear industry also pose a pollution hazard, although the vast majority of this waste is stored or sealed with the intention that it will not reach the environment. The low-level waste which is disposed of by burial consists largely of clothing and other materials from the medical services. This material has been produced as a by-product of medical treatment and usually emits lower levels of radiation than certain rocks which occur naturally at many places on the earth's surface.

Even processes which appear to be environmentally friendly can emit products with undesirable effects. As an example, the burning of wood is known to release polyaromatic hydrocarbons which are carcinogenic, as well as relatively large quantities of carbon dioxide which contributes to the greenhouse effect. A second example is that the use of unleaded petrol may result in increased emissions of simple aromatic hydrocarbons, the effects of which are still the subject of debate and controversy.

Although any of the problems outlined above could be said to constitute an environmental crisis, the perturbation of the global troposphere is likely to have the most serious impact. It is important to realise that ending the perturbation of the global troposphere is effectively impossible. Whilst bans on their production will allow the gradual decomposition of atmospheric halocarbons, with the ozone layer thereafter returning gradually to its natural state, the perturbation of the troposphere has no single cause. Changes here are closely linked to our lifestyle, our energy consumption and global food production, and these are all factors which will prove extremely difficult to change.[8] Moreover, this is a situation which threatens to escalate rapidly in the near future, even if we control emissions of nitrogen oxides and sulphur oxides from power-stations and exhaust emissions from motor-vehicles in Europe and North America.[9] The additional pollution produced in other countries as they adopt so-called western-style industrial and transport practices could far exceed the present emissions from Europe and North America. It is possible that the world cannot cope with the by-products of the present human population, irrespective of its ability to provide the resources of fuel and food which this population needs. Such a threat demands not only a scientific and technological response but also a theological response if our theology is to be relevant to the world in which we live.

1.3 The Theological Context

The perturbation of the global troposphere poses a serious and growing long-term threat to life on this planet. It also emphasises the relationship which exists between humanity and virtually all other living species. It is therefore relevant to identify this situation as the context for the present theology, although most of what follows relates equally to other ecological and environmental issues.

All theology is contextual in as much as it needs to reinterpret the Christian truth for each new generation[10]. What has traditionally been seen as normative in Christian terms has largely been the product of white, middle-class, western thought: the so-called North-Atlantic context. The Taiwanese theologian Choan-Seng Song, who is interested in the assimilation of Christianity into Eastern culture, has noted that the Asian rejection of Christianity is largely a rejection of Western culture rather than of Christianity itself.[11] It is a rejection both of 'North Atlantic Theology' and of the popular perception of the scientific world view which has developed in this region of the world.[12] Theologies which have subsequently been labelled as contextual, such as that of Song himself, were only developed because their local insights had not been taken seriously in other theological systems and thought.[13] Such contextual considerations can encompass prayer, spirituality, worship and Bible-study as well as theological discourse. However, considering God in a particular context (as opposed to through metaphysics or by speculation) also has the advantage of expressing the truth that God is not only transcendent but that He is also immanent and involved with the daily process of living in the world. This is the belief which found particular expression and revelation in Christianity in the Incarnation of Jesus Christ. Through the Incarnation, God's Being is revealed in a particular context (that of human life and existence), by His own action and initiative.[14]

In his theological analysis of global needs, the Sri Lankan theologian Tissa Balasuriya has considered the whole world as his context (a global context) resulting in what he termed a planetary theology.[15] Throughout his writings he persistently raises the issue of whether the traditional expression of Christianity prevents it from exerting a liberating influence where this influence is needed. Ian Barbour, Professor of Science, Technology and Society in Minnesota, has asked the related question as to whether a single religious paradigm (that is, the total of the beliefs, lifestyle and academic study associated with a particular religion) can be valid on a world-wide basis.[16] In response to Barbour, it can be argued that if there is truth in the Christian gospel, in the revelation of the Word of God, then that truth is still valid if we move a few thousand miles, albeit that it may need to be expressed in a different way. If we are concerned with a problem which faces the whole world, then the whole world also needs to be our context. This point has been taken up by Vincent Donovan who spent many years working with the Masai in East Africa. He has reflected that as Christianity claims to be a global religion, it needs to take account of people of all nations and cultures if its theology is to address their situation.[17] This has religious consequences which extend beyond formal theology. Both the Anglican and the Roman Catholic Churches are discovering that it is their membership from the Two-Thirds World, rather than the traditional 'Christian West' which is now setting the agenda.[18] It is also true that advances in global communications and the speed of travel demand a global perspective.

The major challenges for global theologies will be problems which have global proportions or consequences. In his address to the sixth World Council of Churches (WCC), the Indian theologian and bishop Paul Verghase (Bishop Gregorios) identified four such areas of concern. These were Nuclear technology, Biotechnology, Ecological issues and Global injustice.[19] The present study addresses the third of these issues and carries the premise that the earth will only support human life if we care for it and interact with it in an appropriate manner, and do not exploit it beyond certain limits which are a part of its inbuilt nature. The present context also suggests that this might be a theology of liberation, since it is concerned for the whole of creation on this planet, in a context where much of it is under threat.[20] This particular description also serves to remind us that the present theology should suggest a commitment to action and change if its conclusions and results are to be meaningful. If theology is to have any significance or importance, then it must affect the life and direction of the Church locally, whilst remembering that this effect cannot be imposed.

The environmental crisis can too easily be seen only in a

North-Atlantic context, since this region is the present source of most of the atmospheric pollution. The unfortunate implication is that this crisis can seem of little relevance to the Two-Thirds World. This situation has already occurred in discussions concerning controls on the production and use of halocarbons. There is little incentive to implement changes which prevent diseases of middle-age and old-age in those countries where the majority of the population dies before it reaches these stages of life. This is particularly the case when these changes would lower the chance of the population reaching such an age. An example of this problem concerned the rapid phasing out of chlorofluorocarbon refrigerants on a global scale at a time when new replacements were only available in those countries which could afford the higher cost of the alternatives. A similar approach to theology would remove the global context which such theology requires in order to be credible. Anyone truly wishing to adopt a planetary context needs therefore to realise that global problems affect not only the whole human race, but the whole of the life on this planet. The theology which is presented here must take this factor into account.

The approach adopted will be to consider the world as God's creation, the crisis as being caused by human misuse of this creation, and the solution as being seen in terms of a theology of redemption and salvation. What exactly we mean when we state that the world is God's creation will be considered in chapter three. During the development of these ideas, particular attention will be paid to the doctrine of the Trinity and the insights which can be gained from this expression of Christian belief. In so doing, it will also be necessary to examine the language which we use to describe God and the ways in which this can influence our approach to the crisis. Finally, we shall consider the consequences of these studies for the ecclesiology and liturgy of the Church.

1.4 The Theological Method

The method used in the present theological discussion is to apply traditional Christian doctrine within the context under consideration. This approach accepts biblical criticism and the insights of modern theology, but always as they apply within the context of tradition. It always asks whether any suggested changes are necessary or whether they are flights of fancy or merely change for the sake of change. This is similar to the way in which Barbour has described the development of scientific research programmes. He claims that scientific thought consists of a core set of ideas or beliefs to which are then added a larger number of modifiable auxiliary ideas.[21]

It is important to realise that this theological method does not take Christian doctrine as a fixed set of precepts all of which have to be forcibly applied in every situation. Rather, the situation or context sets the agenda by producing a series of questions and these questions are then answered by the application of the relevant doctrines. The effectiveness of these answers is a measure of the relevance of the Christian faith in the present day. The present contention is that Christian Theology contains a richness and depth which is able to address the issues of contemporary society without departing from the basic tenets of Christian belief.

Vincent Donovan has noted that Christ's coming afresh to a culture in this way condemns its bad traits, but also welcomes its high peaks of insight and its ideals.[22] Jesus himself did this with Judaism, and the early Christian communities had to address the questions which arose within Graeco-Roman culture. A similar process occurred in the British Isles when the Celtic Christian tradition emerged from the application of Christian beliefs to the pagan religious practices then present in Britain. In the present day we are called on to do the same with our own culture.

Because it is open to the world and is prepared to incorporate newer developments when necessary, this method is not fundamentally conservative in its approach. However, there is a balance to be achieved with the opposite problem which is that dialogue with the world can produce results which are unpredictable and which may distort the Christian faith.[23] The defence against this possible corruption of Christian belief, is that any dialogue in which we engage has to be real. When we are involved in such discussions it is all too easy to reduce our position to one in which we only listen and in which we contribute neither our own views and beliefs, nor those of the tradition to which we belong, with anything like the same force as do the people with whom we are speaking. We need to rediscover our own truths as well as to discover those of others. There is therefore a balance – a tension – to be maintained between being true to our own faith and being open to the world. We should not lightly dispense with that which has always been a part of our tradition, but only with those parts which have been accretions and which are the result of cultural expression and re-expression through the centuries. Indeed, we might need to rediscover the truth of our own tradition.

Contextual theology done in this way is clearly related to what the German born theologian and philosopher Paul Tillich referred to as 'The Method of Correlation'; the way in which theology answers the questions which result from our real life situation.[24] Tillich described this correlation as being a method which makes an analysis of the human situation from which existential questions arise and then demonstrates that the symbols traditionally associated with the Christian message provide the answers to those questions. The cultural context is therefore provided by the question which the answer must address, and the Christian perspective is provided by the content of the answer. The way in which Tillich described this theological method is of particular interest to us in the present work, because the five correlations which form the basis of his Systematic Theology are directly relevant to our current subject matter, even though we shall not be using them explicitly.

Tillich's first correlation was that in which the question of human finitude is answered by the existence of God.[25] This answer is implicitly assumed in the present work, for the work would not have been undertaken in the first place without the making of the divine supposition. The answer is also provided in the consideration of the doctrine of creation which occurs in the first sections of chapters two to four, as well as by the discussion of salvation and suffering in the latter chapter.

The second correlation posed the question of human existential estrangement together with Tillich's interpretation of Original Sin[26], and answered this with the doctrine of the Incarnation. There are parallels to this in the present work. Chapter two addresses the ecological crisis which can be described in terms of the estrangement of creation, whilst chapter three examines the nature of the creation which is estranged. Chapter four attempts to answer these problems by considering the second person of the Trinity. These correlations also involve the theme of suffering.

Tillich's third correlation was concerned with the issue of the ambiguities which exist in life and found its answer in the indwelling presence of the Holy Spirit. In the present work chapters three and four address the issue of how we might describe God's involvement with and within creation, whilst chapter five moves on to consider the doctrine of The Trinity and how this is related to our conclusions.

The fourth correlation looked for an answer to the limitations to human rationality and the ambiguity which exists in human reason. Here, Tillich formulated his answers in terms of divine revelation. This issue appears here in chapter six when we consider how we are able to use human terminology to talk (or write) about God, and the way in which we need to be prepared to receive the answers from God Himself.

The fifth and final correlation analysed the historical problems of human existence and provided answers in terms of the Kingdom of God. Here this is expressed in chapter four, where the purpose of ongoing continuous historical time and its relationship with the eschaton (the end of time and this world) is discussed. It also occurs in chapters seven and eight where there is a discussion of the way in which the Church can respond to the current crisis and the way in which worship is related to these themes. This whole subject is central to our understanding of the way in which God can be involved with the creation.

This outline of the themes in Tillich's Systematic Theology does more than illustrate the method of correlation. These five correlations, which emerged from the questions of human finitude and estrangement, can clearly be restated to address the context of a creation which is under threat. Tillich's theology, which was developed to respond to the human situation, bears a close thematic similarity to a theology developed for the whole of creation.

Christianity does not need to use new philosophical ideas to affirm the immanent presence of God or His affirmation of creation. The Christian Doctrine of the Trinity protects both the immanence and the transcendence of God, through the transcendent Father, the incarnate Son, and the Holy Spirit who indwells the created order. God is thus both other than the created order, takes the created order to Himself, and can indwell both humanity and the rest of the creation, without any need to move beyond the basic Christian doctrine. Christian worship has traditionally been worship of God the Holy Trinity and this should therefore be our starting point. We should only doubt the efficacy of The Trinity if it proves to be incompatible with what we experience in our lives or what we discover about God (this point is discussed further in chapter five). This approach implies that we need to relearn traditional Christian teaching if we are to proceed with our investigation. We can only attempt to respond to questions using traditional Christian doctrines if we understand these doctrines in the first place. Taking this argument further, we could deduce that our care for the world and the realisation of the Kingdom of God needs to be balanced by the expectation of the eschaton and an understanding of how this is related to time and space.

An understanding of time is important if we are to do our theology in the modern world, where so much scientific understanding is underpinned by the concept of time and where time is therefore part of the context which we must address. The historical movement of Christianity from the past to the future is in marked distinction to religions which perceive time as circular or repetitive. Only in the historical approach can we ever hope to reach the eschaton, and we need to understand time if we are to speak constructively on this subject and to ask the question as to what are the implications of the eschaton for an estranged creation? These are issues which need to be explored in the present theological discussion.

The present work is not another attempt to produce a 'green theology'. The Christian belief in the creative God is fully consistent with a concern for the environment. Rather, this work is an attempt to ask what our traditions, beliefs and religious practices have to say in the present situation as well as an examination of what we might need to relearn about these beliefs and practices if we are to see their true significance. If the results of this questioning are of any importance then they will also have implications for the ways in which we understand and conduct the worship and organisation of the Church. Above all, this work is trying to say something about how a Christian can understand the significance of God in the world today as well as how he can understand his own relationship to that world.

Notes

1. Examples of such publications range from popular accounts, such as those of McDonagh and Ambler, through studies of models for God in an ecological, nuclear age (McFague), to an ecological doctrine of creation (Moltmann, 1985).
2. E.g. Hough (1988); Buckley-Golder; Cowling.
3. E.g. DoE (1987a); Hough and Derwent (1987).
4. E.g. WMO; DoE (1987b).
5. E.g. WMO; Dickinson & Cicerone; Ramanathan et.al.
6. E.g. Hough and Derwent (1990); Isaksen & Hov; Volz & Kley.
7. It is important to realise that like most of these issues, the pollution of surface waters by nitrates and pesticides from farming is a complex issue. Without the use of fertilizers and pesticides the yields from many farms would fall dramatically.
8. E.g. Hough (1991).
9. Hough & Derwent (1990).
10. Tillich (1978a) pp.3–8. Tillich also noted that whilst making this reinterpretation, neither the truth nor the situation should be obliterated.
11. Song pp.7–9.
12. Barbour pp.76f.
13. E.g. Balasuriya, pp.13ff.
14. Peacocke pp.201ff.
15. Balasuriya esp. pp.13–16.
16. Barbour pp.57f.
17. Donovan pp.5–8.
18. The term 'Two-thirds World' reflects the fact that two thirds of the world's population lives in the area being considered and avoids the problem that the term 'Third-World' can seem to imply third-rate.
19. The text of the address is conveniently reproduced on pp.400ff of Gill.
20. McFague pp.xivf discusses this aspect of liberation theology.
21. Barbour pp.60ff.
22. Donovan p.126.
23. Donovan pp.124ff.
24. Tillich (1978a) pp.59ff.
25. In his systematic theology, Tillich often uses the word existence with a

particular specialist meaning. In this instance the word is used in a very general sense with no particular philosophical connotations.

26. As discussed below in section 2.3, Tillich also distinguished Sin itself from sins or moral misdeeds. Throughout this book, 'Original Sin' will always be spelt with capital letters in order to be consistent with the capitalisation of the word Sin when used to denote Sin itself.

Chapter 2

Christianity and Environmental Crisis

In chapter one the discussion included an examination of the environmental crisis which faces the Earth. In particular, the pollution of the global atmosphere by the human population was identified as the key element in the present crisis. If we are to examine this crisis from a Christian perspective and within the framework of traditional Christian doctrine, then the most important topic which we must examine is that of how both humanity and the Church are to understand their roles in relation to the rest of the created order. What is the place of the human species in the world and what is the role of the Church in creation? For the moment we will accept the givenness of creation and examine the causes of the present problem. We will move on to discuss the nature of creation itself in more detail in chapter three.

2.1 The Environment as Creation

The conclusion that the present environmental crisis is the result of human exploitation and misuse of the natural environment or creation, inevitably leads to a consideration of the early chapters of the book of Genesis. It is here that we find the traditional Judaeo-Christian religious accounts and understanding of our origins and of our place within the rest of creation. This is the divine scheme for the ordering of the world.

In the usual reading of these chapters, the first of these accounts, from the Priestly source, carries the divine edict that men are to have dominion over all living creatures and are to subdue the earth.[1] The second account, from the Yahwist, is usually taken to include the implication that Sin, here described as the knowledge of good and evil, consists in man's striving for that knowledge and power which properly belong to God.[2] A further reference to this second theme can be seen in the account of the Tower of Babel (Genesis Ch.11 vv1-9).

These ideas are not far removed from the injunction in the Ten Commandments, or Decalogue, that man shall not make any graven image or bow down to and worship such an image.[3] The production of images, as objects for human worship, was linked to the desire to control and manipulate God, which is again a striving for a knowledge and power which rightly belong to God Himself. The same considerations apply to the way in which the Deuteronomic writers and prophets such as Hosea condemned local worship at Hill Shrines because these practices originated in the worship of pagan or nature gods. However, as the Old Testament Scholar Walter Moberly has observed, they did not deny the validity of this form of worship for the Patriarchs, such as Abraham and Jacob, who knew no better.[4] It had come to be realised that the God who is behind everything that is, cannot be worshipped in any meaningful or adequate way when He is identified with images which were constructed by human beings. The idea of God as creator tends to separate the World from God and, as such, God is both beyond the images which we make of Him and is greater than His creation.

St. Paul made a similar point when he wrote the first chapter of his letter to the Romans. Here, in verses 18-25, he notes the foolishness of men in abandoning worship of the true creator for the worship of idols which they had made with their own hands. For Paul, this was the root cause of the corrupted human state; namely that men worshipped creation rather than the creator God.[5] They usurped God's power and took it to themselves. Moreover, there was no excuse which could be offered on their behalf, because the whole creation shows the nature and presence of God.[6] The significance of these words was not lost on the early Fathers of the Church, and we find them echoed by Athanasius in his writing on the incarnation.[7] He noted that although the evidence for God was present in the world for all people to see, it was persistently ignored as men turned from God to the creation and to the works of their own hands.

However, this problem is not simply one of usurping God's power and position and of failing to worship the one true God. It has consequences which are considerably more important. In reaction against worship of the creation and in an attempt to focus the attention instead upon God the creator, there can develop a tendency to distance God from His creation and to produce the vision of a transcendent God who is wholly separate from the world and who therefore plays no part in it. It has been argued that the separation produced by this crude form of dualism and the teaching that the physical world was not to be worshipped or reverenced, led to human exploitation of the natural environment.[8] There could be no harm in such exploitation, so it was claimed, because nature is not divine – it is not where God is to be found. The world is therefore available to be explored by scientific methods and exploited by human technology.

The contemporary British theologian Janet Martin Soskice has noted that for a whole generation, much of the dialogue between science and theology has been concentrated on how we are to understand the Biblical accounts of creation whilst living in a scientific age. The question which is addressed in this dialogue is that of how can we reconcile science and the first three chapters of the book of Genesis? However, Soskice makes the important point that the Biblical accounts are not concerned with where the world came from and what it was like, but rather who it came from and what kind of creation it is.[9] The issue should therefore not be what can we do to the world if God is not present within it, but rather what can we do in the world if it was created by God. It is important to realise that the common approach, in which God is assumed to be absent from creation, makes an a priori assumption about the supremacy of human reason. It fails to ask what the biblical accounts might tell us about ourselves and our relationships with the rest of that creation.

It is notable that the eminent Swiss theologian Karl Barth,

for all his desire to re-express and re-establish the transcendent power of God breaking in upon humanity from above, could still note that man had failed to understand the implications of God calling His creation good. 'The Creation of God carries with it the Yes of God to that which He creates..... What takes shape in it is the goodness of God'.[10] Barth's contemporary and fellow-countryman, Emil Brunner, similarly noted that man loses his true humanity when he believes that this identity consists of the mastery of nature; that if man loses sight of God, his position in the world becomes perverted to a state in which he exploits nature.[11] The Irish theologian Gabriel Daly expresses this problem in terms of the idea that man has reached the stage where his powers over nature are sufficient to allow him to force the pace and to progress at a rate which is faster than evolution. He sees the problem as lying not in this human power itself – for this power was given by God – but rather in the abuse of this power. He believes that we need a deeper appreciation of what it is to be truly human.[12]

Jurgan Moltmann traces this attitude to the influence of philosophers such as Emmanuel Kant who, so Moltmann argues, stressed the knowledge which could be gained by man if he treated the world as wholly separate from himself and as the object of his studies, without the presence of any element of subjectivity.[13] We could summarise this position as being one in which the human race has failed to realise that it exists in relationship with the rest of creation and that in its activities it seeks to control the world in such a way that humanity decides what will happen in the future. This human action to remove the range of options available for the future is what Moltmann has termed the 'closing of open systems', a description in which he uses language borrowed from thermodynamics.[14] This concept of 'open-systems' is important for our understanding of salvation and we shall return to it in chapter four.

However, Moltmann's use of the word 'man' in his writings, suggests that this separation between the human race and the environment is a universal condition. This contrasts with the tradition in far-eastern cultures and those of many tribal peoples which still see man as a part of the natural environment and in constant interaction with all that is about him.

Perhaps the truth is that when humanity loses touch with its true identity, as being created and living in relationship with the rest of creation, it also loses touch with its true responsibilities within and to that creation. As long ago as the 1940s, Tillich noted that humanity had lost the ability to communicate and live with nature.[15] Indeed, this whole subject is closely related to what Tillich described as 'Belief-ful Realism' – the answer to the question of the relationship between God and the World. Realism, because we are concerned with the real world and not with conjecture. Belief-ful, because this is an attitude born of an approach which places God in the centre.[16]

This discussion can also be related to the use of the word 'environment' and the debate concerning its meaning. The suggestion has been made that since this word finds its origins in the concept of surrounding (i.e. environing), it indicates a state of mind which views creation or nature as something which is set over and against humanity, something of which we are not a part and which surrounds and envelops us. This would be the understanding of primitive cultures and religions. In reaction, humanity sees the need to react by 'environing' the creation – to surround and control it instead. However, the issue which we need to face is not so much one of whether we are surrounded or whether we can surround and subdue, but rather that of how we can work with that in which we live; how the mutual symbiotic relationship between humanity and the world is to be lived out in practice. Soskice has observed that, for these reasons, it may be preferable to use the word 'Creation' rather than 'Environment', provided that we acknowledge that we are a part of that creation.[17] Such a use also serves to remind us of the higher authority which lies behind the universe and which is responsible for its creation.

2.2 Is Christianity to Blame?

At first sight, the suggestion that the pertinent question is one of how humanity can work with the rest of creation rather than controlling or exploiting it, can appear to be contrary to Judaeo-Christian principles. The most obvious instance of such a principle would appear to be the human dominion over creation which is described in chapter one of Genesis and the first four verses of chapter two. Christianity has often been blamed for the human misuse of nature and this blame has been placed in particular on this account of creation.

This thesis was given its classic expression in an article by Lynn White in 1967.[18] White argued that western people feel superior to nature, contemptuous of it and willing to use it for their slightest whim. He blamed this on what he perceived as the Christian axiom that nature has no reason for existence other than to serve men and that science and technology are corrupted by this Christian arrogance. White's understanding of Christian tradition, which is summed up in the translation that man is told by God to 'subdue the Earth', ignores the full implications of the later passage in the same chapter in which God describes the whole of the creation as 'good'.

When the theology of 'green issues' is discussed in a general setting, Christianity is often attacked on two accounts: first for promoting a negative attitude towards a supposedly fallen world and secondly for being anthropocentric.[19] The criticism is made that if human beings believe that they are made in the image of God, then they perceive themselves as superior to the rest of the creation. This view is reinforced by the theory that it was the presence of the Christian culture which allowed the rise of science and hence its technological applications. It is claimed that pagan or Earth religions, which revere the natural order, do not make this mistake: they do not see men as being inherently superior to the rest of the creation.

The criticism that Christianity is to blame for the present environmental crisis has not gone unchallenged, with authors such as Arthur Peacocke, a British biochemist who later became a theologian, noting that exploitation of nature was absent from Christian thought for much of its history and that it is not a necessary part of Judaeo-Christian belief.[20] He notes that tree stripping in the Mediterranean Basin predates the period of the Jewish prophets and that Christian practice varies widely. Rather than seeing the rise of technology in the West as dependent upon Christianity, Hendry sees its late emergence (compared, for instance, with that in China) as a mystery which could possibly be explained by a popular piety which regarded nature with mistrust due to a supposed malevolence, based on the doctrine of the Fall.[21]

These views are by no means universal, and the rise of science is still widely attributed to Christianity and to the Christian view of creation, although this need not necessarily lead to exploitation. Ian Barbour notes that science may have arisen in a Christian milieu because, like Greek thought, it saw the World as orderly and intelligible, so that it could be investigated and described.[22] This view is supported by John Polkinghorne a former Professor of Mathematical Physics who has become a leading writer on the relationship between science and religion.[23] However, unlike Greek thought, this orderliness was contingent, not a necessity, so that it had to be investigated by experiment and observation rather than being deduced from first principles. In other words, it was the belief that the world was created and not the belief that humanity held dominion over the Earth which led to the development of scientific thought.

It is also important to note that the subject of pure science and that of technology are actually quite different to each other. Science, in its pure form, is a searching after knowledge whereas technology is the practical application of that knowledge. Science often retains a romantic element and a sense of mystery. A good example of this in the present context concerns the discovery of the so-called 'hole' in the ozone layer over Antarctica. This hole was discovered by scientists based on the ice and using simple instruments over which they had minute to minute control, rather than by complex satellite based systems which used a great deal of applied technology.

In earlier centuries, science was seen as an exploration of creation which, in turn, was thought to produce a grander view of God. It can therefore be argued that Science is based on the study of the divine creation, in contrast to The Arts which is the study of the products of humanity. Irrespective of the historical processes involved, Moltmann is surely correct in stating that science and theology now need to work together for a greater ecological awareness,[24] a thought which we will examine further below.

Janet Martin Soskice has defended the place of anthropocentrism within Christianity with some force. Her argument is that if we are made in the image of God, then we are in some way a mystery and are ourselves not fully comprehensible.[25] This idea works in two ways. Without the concept of our being made in God's image, then we lose our sense of responsibility and our being accountable for our actions to some higher authority. Secondly, we lose our notion of the worth of human individuals. Soskice here notes that:

'The death of God will not, as Nietzsche thought, result in the glorification of man, but rather will take from women and men any claim they have to be reverenced as participating in the divine economy. Without God and without the sanctity of the person made in the image of God, women and men will become not gods but mere objects to manipulate in a world of manipulable objects.'

Soskice goes on to make the point that this would result in a situation in which, for example, policies on selective infanticide would become acceptable.

The problem is not caused by anthropocentrism as such, but rather by its misuse and by age-old problems such as greed, pride, jealousy, avarice, anger and covetousness; human flaws which damage the divine image in which we are made. It is a great mystery to be made in the image of God and there is nothing wrong in holding such a belief. It only becomes a problem when the belief becomes flawed and humanity is placed at the centre rather than God and then attempts to draw all things to itself and to take control for its own ends. Being made in the image of God and being of worth for this reason does not imply that human beings are divine and are therefore equal with God. A creative and caring anthropocentrism within creation need not be a problem, provided that we acknowledge that it is God who is at the true centre of all.

A major part of the problem facing Christianity at the present time is that it has, to a large extent, lost touch with the scientific view of the origins of the world and of life. Although much of the recent dialogue between science and theology has been constructive, as shown in the review by Barbour,[26] this dialogue has had little in common with Biblical theology. In popular opinion, Christianity is still perceived as being 'out of touch' with the scientific world-view; a perception which can be exploited by those who wish to adopt an anti-christian stance. This apparent split between theology and science has its origins in the mid-nineteenth century controversy concerning the evolutionary theories which were then being developed. Here, a naive form of dualism was used against Darwin, in which physical aspects of nature were assigned to science and anything concerned with mind or spirit (the human preserve) was the concern of religion. At the same time, biblical fundamentalism and a misunderstanding of the creation narratives resulted in the lack of a credible Christian cosmology for an increasingly scientific age.

As long ago as the fourth century, Augustine of Hippo noted the ridiculous nature of Christian claims to refute the results of scientific studies by reference to scripture. How, he asked, are people to believe our teaching on the resurrection of the dead, eternal life and the Kingdom of Heaven, if we make bizarre claims about the physical world. Augustine realised that Science and Theology often deal with different questions, or with different aspects of the same question, when he noted that what science could prove, can be shown as not contrary to scripture. Moreover, many of the theological objections to evolution were really a facade for the feelings of affront felt by those who held strongly anthropocentric views and who found these to be incompatible with theories of evolution. As a result, developments in the theological understanding of creation were largely ignored at the time when scientific understanding was increasing most rapidly.

There can be little doubt that western Christianity has a strong anthropocentric nature and that the recent growth in theological concern for the environment is a welcome counter-balance to this attitude. Too much attention has been paid to Genesis Ch.1 vv28-30, whilst neglecting not only the rest of the same chapter, but also John Ch.3 v16 and Romans Ch.8 vv18-25 with their important statements of God's love for the whole created order and the promise of its redemption. Yet, if we are to move away from the concept of exploitative domination, we need to ensure that we do not move to the other extreme and start to worship the creation rather than the creator. Nor need anthropocentrism itself be intrinsically bad or irrevocably linked to the exploitation of the world. If the

Priestly account in Genesis chapter one places the world into human care, then this is surely a view which is both anthropocentric and also implicitly directed against the exploitation of nature.

The two extremes in position which can result from a theological stance either for or against religious anthropocentrism have been well summarized by Emil Brunner.[27] Brunner saw Sin as perverting human nature in one of two directions. The first consisted in self-deification, exemplified by the exploitation of nature, whilst the second consisted in a deification of the world, which we could term nature-worship or pantheism. Neither of these positions is true to the historical tradition of the Christian faith. A modified anthropocentrism in which nature is neither deified nor exploited is clearly required, but this will not in itself be sufficient if each individual of the human species is concerned solely with his or her personal salvation. Christianity is not (or should not be) an individualistic cult. Rather it should be a faith in which the destiny of the whole world and the whole of the human species is of vital concern. Although the Bible does not contain a systematic theology of nature it does contain God's affirmation that in the beginning His creation was good, as well as St. Paul's expression that the whole of creation is awaiting its salvation (Romans Ch.8 vv18-25). This concern for the whole of the creation, rather than for the individual, is an outworking of the relationships which exist in the Kingdom of Heaven.

Despite recent progress, it is still open to question as to whether Christianity (and western Christianity in particular) can escape from its common image of domination and misplaced anthropocentrism. In particular, can it do this without falling into the trap of nature worship and pantheism? Tillich noted that we need to maintain a balance whereby we appreciate the natural beauty of the world, but also realise the natural tragedy which exists within nature.[28] Whilst caring for the world, we must not idolise or sentimentalise it, but rather accept that like us it has its problems and its violence. We also need to avoid turning Christianity into a single-issue faith, as would happen if doctrine was determined solely by environmental issues, and instead consider it as a whole.

The way in which popular Christianity can take a part of

Christian Doctrine and turn it into something which assumes the proportions of the whole is demonstrated by the way in which it can place undue emphasis on one particular aspect of God at the expense of others. An example of this is the weight which often seems to be given to an almighty patriarchal image of God, which not only ignores the insights into God which we gain through Jesus Christ and The Holy Spirit, but which is also a caricature of God the Father. A further example of this difficulty is furnished by Christians who devote most of their attention to Jesus at the expense of the Father and the Holy Spirit. There appears to be an innate tendency inherent in many if not all church bodies to place undue emphasis on one person of the Trinity at the expense of the others. There is also a tendency to oversimplify, to believe that the Christian faith can be completely explained and understood. This simplification results in a loss of the sense of mystery and awe and renders faith vulnerable to changing circumstances.

This problem is related to what the English ethicist and writer Helen Oppenheimer has described as the human lack of comprehension of our humanities own createdness and the concomitant loss of the wanting, longing and striving character of our love for and to God. In this respect she notes the teaching of St. Augustine, that if we lose our longing then we will lapse into silence.[29] If we can recognise our createdness and our ultimate dependence on God, not just intellectually but deep within ourselves, then we can move beyond a dangerous and misplaced anthropocentrism to a more positive approach. Here we can enter into a relationship of giving and responding to the rest of creation as well as being more honest in our relationship with God. Indeed, Oppenheimer notes that such giving and responding may well be linked to the love which exists within the Holy Trinity itself.[30] In the words of the shorter catechism, we are called on to 'Glorify God and enjoy Him forever.'

It is the contention of this work that both the Christian Church and its theology can move in a direction which will enable them to avoid the problems we have identified above, and which will also enable them to speak with greater authority on the environmental crisis which we face. Central to this movement needs to be a continuing development of a theology of creation. This development needs to involve the concern which God has for the whole of His creation and not just for the human element within it and to do this without denying the unique place which humanity occupies in the created order. This approach also needs to take in the different but related questions of who does creation come from and what it means to be created, whilst avoiding an obsession with mechanistic ideas of how creation occurred.

The Church and its teachers need to pay attention to the perennial problem of balancing the recognition of Divine transcendence with that of Divine immanence and of holding the two together. God cannot be totally other than the world or He would have no interest in it, nor can He be wholly within the world if He is to be regarded as possessing a 'personal' nature. If God is regarded as being wholly within the world, then to retain His personhood is to deny his divinity and to retain His divinity is to identify him with the creation and thereby to lose his personhood to a belief in pantheism.

Popular discussions about God have often made the error of stressing His transcendence at the expense of His immanence, usually with the intention of emphasising the difference between God and human beings. On the other hand, liberal theologians have often made the opposite error and played down the transcendent aspect of God. This is a subject which will be examined further in chapter three. As has been indicated before, our understanding of the Trinity is crucial in developing this argument and its relevance needs to be explored and expressed more fully. Indeed, The Trinity is largely ignored in popular piety and poorly understood in popular religious thought. How can we hope to formulate an adequate Christian response to any situation if we do not understand this fundamental aspect of Christian doctrine and belief? If we believe in a realist God who is both Creator and Triune, then this trinitarian nature should make itself manifest in our understandings of creation and in our relationships with the creator. If we are unable or unwilling to make such a connection, then we are implicitly doubting either God's trinitarian nature and/or His reality.[31]

The other traditional doctrine of which we can also lose sight, perhaps because it is out of fashion in much liberal theology is that of Original Sin. To speak of Original Sin is not simply to speak in a figurative way, but rather to describe something which causes actual disruption in the world. This has already entered in our discussion of misplaced anthropocentrism, but we shall explore its importance further in section 2.3 below. The Church needs to retain hold of the truths which are expressed within this doctrine for they shed important light on the way in which we can understand the present crisis and the human misuse of the world. If we can understand our present predicament in terms of The Fall, then a distinctive Christian response is already available through the doctrine of the atonement. This is the second Tillichian correlation which we noted in chapter one. The Cross was not the solution to an unexpected emergency but a part of God's eternal plan. There is something about human nature which made it essential.

2.3 The Relationship with Society

Western society may have more of a problem than Christianity in dealing with environmental concerns. This is a difficulty which exists both within society itself and also in its attitude to a world in which progress is increasingly measured in terms of technological achievement and in which individualism is increasingly dominant. As long ago as 1975, a report associated with the Doctrine Commission of the Church of England noted that accepting God as Creator implied that we should work with God and that this meant that we had to turn away from grasping and from greed.[32] In the following decade, Moltmann noted that whereas man was once surrounded (or environed) by overwhelming nature (in which context the command to subdue or to environ the earth could make sense), he is now overwhelmed by his own products and a bureaucracy and technology that have got out of hand. Now man is a master of nature but a slave of his own works.[33] We are captives of the system which we have produced.

Western society also has problems with its image of God. In this society, the popular conception of what is meant by God is indeed the dominant, remote, transcendent, patriarchal figure which we noted in section 2.2 above. Whilst it is true that this is an unwitting caricature of Christian belief, it is also one which was encouraged by Scholastic theologians. In as much as this image is unhelpful in the present global context and is also a false representation of Christian Doctrine, it is a problem which the Church needs to address if it is to speak to those people who reject Christianity because they believe that this is what it teaches. The rejection of Christianity through the rejection of this false god leaves society without a religious ideal and creates a vacuum into which various images can be placed as man once more creates idols of various kinds.

Although the Church must not lose sight of the fuller implications of the doctrine of creation, nor dilute its message, it is more relevant in the present context to consider what it means 'to be created' rather than to debate the mechanics of how the act of creation worked.[34] We need to consider the gift of life and the mystery of individual persons, together with their practical consequences, rather than debate the extent to which the first three chapters of Genesis are to be understood in a literal sense.

Unfortunately, the increase in environmental concern which has occurred in western society is inextricably interwoven with what Daly calls 'cunning self-interest'. The concern is often centred on the survival of humanity, rather than on the welfare of the whole of creation. According to Daly, 'Genuine ecological concern is a spiritual condition' and the ecological responsibilities of humanity stem from our true human condition of thought, free-will and power.[35] The necessary change in perspective is intimately linked to our view of our place in the world. If we believe that the world is, in some way, the creation of God, then this is a religious and a theological issue. It implies that we need to consider what we mean by creation and how we are to understand its relationship with God.

Part of the problem would appear to be a consequence of the loss of the human sense of awe. All too often we fail to grasp the splendour of the surroundings in which we live, dismissing them in a few seconds before moving on to look at the next view. This belittles both God and His creation as we fail to appreciate the spectacle of that which is around us. We treat the World as a photograph album of two dimensional images to be opened and shut at will. Oppenheimer placed this state of affairs in context by noting that it is as if a child was to work long and hard at something for it then to be dismissed by an adult as 'Very nice dear.'[36] We need to be careful that we do not treat God and the divine creation in the same patronising fashion.

At the root of all these problems lies the fact that modern society has lost touch with the doctrine of Original Sin and rejects the belief that human nature is invariably tainted. Rather than considering Sin in its entirety, it concentrates instead on deciding on whether individual actions are morally right or wrong. There is the inherent implication that human beings have the ability to behave 'correctly' all of the time if only they were to try hard enough. This heresy, known as pelagianism, is what Tillich described as the self-deception of idolatry.[37] Once we attain a certain degree of what we might describe as 'goodness', we reach for divinity and instead commit idolatry and a tragic self-destruction.[38] Pelagianism is a heresy which is always with us. We need to clarify the distinction between Sin itself and sins, seeing the latter as actions which are judged as morally wrong whereas the former is the human state which inevitably manifests itself in the form of the latter.[39] Today, the inherently sinful nature of humanity is manifested in egotistical activities of many kinds which we experience around us, one of which is the idea that the world exists for the benefit of the human species and that our own well-being is the primary consideration. The 'cunning self-interest' of much environmental concern is an example of this problem.

As we noted above, the Church can also fall into this trap and reject the truths which are expressed in the concept of Original Sin. One way of expressing the truth contained in the account of Adam and Eve eating of the tree of the knowledge of good and evil in Genesis chapter three, is to see it as humanity rejecting the idea of divine supremacy (i.e. unbelief), placing itself in the centre (hubris) and then drawing power and control to itself (concupiscence).[40] Having lost sight of God, we look at ourselves and, like Narcissus, place our worship there. Liberal theological tendencies have tended to play down the doctrine of Original Sin and have therefore repeatedly fallen into pelagianism. Theologians such as

Matthew Fox, who reject the idea of Original Sin, would appear to have failed to observe the world around them.[41] Although God affirms the world as His handiwork, things in the world have a tendency to go wrong. This can be seen in human nature as well as in natural disasters and in the diseases which occur throughout the living world. The creation is undoubtedly good and blessed, indeed it is indwelt by the Spirit of God, but this does not mean that it is a utopia.

Recent defences of Pelagius, the British Monk of the late fourth and early fifth centuries after whom the heresy of pelagianism is named, have focused on the goodness of nature and on the fact that Augustine of Hippo, his arch-enemy, is likely to have mis-represented him.[42] In fact, the views of Pelagius himself were much more moderate than the doctrine as it is now stated and it was his followers who put forward the more extreme position which is now inextricably associated with his name. Augustine only developed his full doctrine of Original Sin in reaction to pelagian extremes. Although we now reject much of what Augustine originally wrote on this subject, including the notion that unbaptised babies were condemned to Hell if they should die (Augustine was himself horrified that he had to reach this conclusion), it does seem that human beings have an inherent inability to always do that which is right.

The fact is, that we are far too optimistic of the human potential to do good. We only have to look at the world around us to grasp the awful truth about human nature irrespective of its cause. Although the Old Testament scholar James Barr has expressed serious doubts about whether chapter three of Genesis describes the origin of human sin, finding instead a description of why human beings are mortal, he has no doubts about the presence of Original Sin.[43] Paul Tillich made it clear that whatever the truth of the account in Genesis, Original Sin is a fact of life. There is a gap between ideal human behaviour and what we actually experience in the world. This is sometimes described as alienation: alienation in the sense that we are alienated from our ideal selves, from the world and from God.

The important point to grasp here is that it is the evidence of human behaviour which points to the fact that it is impossible for humanity to behave in an ideal way. This impossibility can be described as the presence of Original Sin or 'fallen nature'.

If we are honest, we know that we can never behave in perfect moral accord or in perfect response to the world in which we live. This is not an a priori argument that humanity is fallen and that individuals therefore commit sins. It is a factual description of what can be seen around us, namely that human individuals inevitably fail in any attempt to live a perfect life. A title can then be given to that state of failure which must, a posteriori, exist. A suitable title is 'Original Sin'.

Although authors such as Polkinghorne are correct to qualify this premise and to distinguish between physical and moral evil, the former being natural disasters and death and the latter the result of conscious human decision, this should not be taken to imply that humanity has the ability to avoid making decisions which result in moral evil.[44] The warning against the idea that utopia is achievable by human activity is found in the very word itself, for 'utopia' is literally ου τοποσ (ou topos – no place) a state which does not exist in the present world. Christianity developed its own warning against the notion that evil has already been finally conquered through its image of the one thousand year reign of Christ followed by the final judgement, a description which can be found in chapter twenty of The Book of Revelation. The speculation as to the need for judgement at the end of this one thousand year reign was a clear sign that evil was not a spent force in the world other than in a particular place or at a special time.

However, although we need to grasp the reality that we will never be able to act in an ideal manner (which is another way of stating that the Kingdom of God cannot be achieved by human endeavour alone) this does not imply that we should abandon all attempts to care for the world. Knowledge that all our best environmental efforts can never completely triumph does not mean that we should stop trying, just as the knowledge that we will fail in any other area of our lives should not prevent us from making the attempt to succeed. We have a vocation to try; but to try without relying totally on our own strength and to try in the knowledge that our success will be limited.

We must also be aware of assuming that the problems of The Church and the problems of society are entirely separate. The Church may well be called to be distinct from society, but at the same time it is also a part of that society. The Church can only be prophetic if it retains some identity with that to which it prophesies. If the environmental crisis is caused by a misplaced anthropocentrism in the human attitude and approach to the world, then it is highly probable that the same human attitude can cause a problem within the Church. Here the crisis occurs in our theology, our beliefs and in our faith itself as we again adopt a misplaced anthropocentrism and place humanity at the centre. We can come to rely on and to worship the products of our own human activity; in this case not the works of our hands but the works of our minds and intellect. In a desperate attempt to be relevant to the modern world we can develop esoteric theologies whilst failing to understand traditional doctrines and how they can and do already answer our questions. Once again we can lose sight of the transcendent God and worship the creation rather than the creator, albeit in a more subtle way than before. Rather than new theologies, we need a restatement of old truths in a way which is relevant to the present day. The real need in both the Church and Society is to develop a true humility – that state in which we truly know our own character and our own place in the creation.

2.4 Some Ethical Considerations

In the previous sections of this chapter we have already adopted an ethical position which considers the human exploitation of the divine creation and makes a statement about Original Sin. In so doing, we have employed a mixture of deontological and teleological arguments. In deontology, actions are regarded as being intrinsically right or wrong and individuals are understood as having particular obligations or duties to those around them. In contrast, teleology states that whether an action is right or wrong is determined by its consequences and that it has no intrinsic ethical value.

In the present deontological arguments, reference has been made to the divine edict that creation is good and that humanity is made in the divine image. The teleological arguments have expressed the desire for the overall good of the creation, albeit that deontological statements of what is ethically correct may underlie the presuppositions of these teleological arguments for the greater common good. Ethical considerations will continue to occur throughout the rest of the work. The intention in this section is therefore not to develop a detailed ethic for the present situation, but rather to consider some of the underlying considerations which will be used in the subsequent chapters.

Whilst there is no intention of denying the above deontological position, this statement that creation is good and that humanity is made in the divine image is not sufficient. It fails to take account of any ongoing divine interaction with the world and it ignores the insights which can be gained through the notion of Heilsgeschichte or Salvation History in which the saving action of God in the life of a people or nation can become clear with hindsight. The historical narratives of the Old Testament make it clear how God was involved in the everyday events of His people. There is a need to explore the implications which this unfolding saga of the history of the people of God has for creation and for our relationship with our surroundings. Indeed, if we are to do justice to the doctrine of the Trinity then we have no alternative but to use this framework, since we have to consider the divine action throughout all time and the redeeming act of the incarnate Word of God as well as the notion of creation in the beginning.

Stanley Hauerwas has noted that Christian ethics begins by calling attention to a narrative in which God deals with creation.[45] Morality is then not an external imposition upon the system, but an integral part of the created narrative. This approach has the advantage that it refuses to separate God and goodness, and thereby exposes the fallacy in the Euthyphro dilemma in which we are asked to decide on whether an action is good because God commands it or whether God commands it because it is good.[46] The whole of the present work is set in the context of such a narrative in which ethics is an integral part of the whole.

If we are then to work in terms of a narrative, this procedure has the further advantage of enabling us to make our approach more specifically Christian. We can place our discussions within the Christian historical narrative and use this as our ongoing theme rather than having to refer back to particular statements fixed at particular points in time and to a creation which occurred not only prior to the incarnation but also prior to human consciousness. We should always be on the guard against the erosion of a distinctive Christian contribution to the argument, for if we are convinced of and interested in the created nature of the world and wish to explore its implications then we must do this from within a religious perspective. We must avoid slipping into arguments of moral philosophy alone, for then our considerations are no longer Christian but abstract – indeed, they are likely to be tainted by some other doctrine without us being aware of the fact. We have to have the courage to make the divine narrative our own. If we can do this, then our ethical stance, which will always be determined at least in part by the narrative of our own life, will also come from that of the divine action within history. If we work within the Christian tradition then this stance will be rooted in the life of Jesus Christ. Moreover, it will be so rooted not through the use of proof texts or the making of salient points, but by our being a part of the ongoing history of the people of God. A history which contains both the biblical narrative and the history of God's people up to the present day.

Hauerwas has noted the refusal of moral philosophers to let Christians be different in their ethical arguments in case this prejudices dialogue between Christians and philosophers.[47] As we have already noted above, this position can all too often lead to a Christian desire not to be different in case this prejudices dialogue. In both cases the resulting dialogue takes place within the bounds of moral philosophy rather than Christianity. We should note Tillich's discussion of the relationship between Theology and Philosophy in which he noted that the two disciplines ask their questions from different standpoints and that genuine dialogue between the two is therefore impossible. Real dialogue has to involve one of these two groups abandoning its viewpoint and only becomes possible on either theological or philosophical territory. It cannot operate in some imaginary area between the two disciplines.[48] If the choice has to be made between risking the dilution of faith and belief or entering into a dialogue then followers of the Christian faith are becoming too fond of taking the latter course. If we accept that

Original Sin is involved in this crisis, then we cannot enter a dialogue in which there is no admission of failure, and in which the desire appears to be an attempt to map out the best way to achieve human utopia. A utopia which Christians know is unobtainable.

Bishop Gregorios has argued that the salient ethical questions to ask in contexts such as our own, concern the origins of life and its purpose – origins which are discussed in terms of intent rather than the mechanism of creation. He sees such considerations as lying beyond the domain of science, which is instead concerned with mechanism. He notes that the distinctive feature of created objects and in particular that of living creatures, is that they display order; that unlike the rest of matter, their formation from their constituent parts would involve a negative entropy change (they display a greater order than do the chemical species from which they are made). Actually, this is an over-simplification, for although the entropy of the living creature may be lower, that of the universe as a whole will have increased. What is true, however, is that whereas the universe as a whole displays an increase in entropy with time (it becomes more disordered), the formation and growth of living creatures displays a local decrease in entropy.

From such a viewpoint, death is the time in the existence of a living creature when the ongoing and local negative change in entropy, upon which life depends, is reversed and a positive change occurs without subsequent and overall reversal. In this way, biological life can be described as overcoming death in the present time and eternal life can be seen as involving a similar decrease in entropy in the future. In this context it is notable that according to the second law of thermodynamics, it is impossible to achieve a negative change in entropy within a closed system and that there always has to be an interaction with the outside of the system for such a change to occur. Even then, the net change for the overall larger system is still positive.

Perhaps the fundamental ethical consideration expressed both within the narrative and in the second law of thermodynamics is that life is a gift and not something which we possess of our own making. Our lower entropy as individuals is only possible as the result of an increase in disorder elsewhere. This is similar to the idea that we are created and that we rely on the sustenance of some thing beyond ourselves. The religious concept of repentance points to a relearning (the literal meaning of the Greek μετανοια) of this truth. If this is the case, then it is impossible to separate the divine covenant made with the human race within human history from the creation of humanity in the first place because both are linked to the narrative of the people of God. The same applies to the other Christian pairing of the cross and the redemption achieved by Jesus Christ. If the Covenant and the cross are separated from history, then they are both reduced to the status of motivators for morality rather than being parts of it. They become external impositions rather than parts of the whole. They deny that God has a direct involvement with the creation, an idea which runs counter to both the Incarnation and the indwelling presence of the Holy Spirit. If we apply this argument to the case of the cross and redemption, then this implies that we are called upon to reject subjective views of the atonement (those in which our personal salvation is based on our own actions) because they verge on being pelagian.

Yet although we are called upon to recognise and to live within the ongoing history of the people of God, this does not mean or imply that we should be passive, sitting by and waiting for the next event to happen. In fact, we are called to do the exact opposite; to search for the living God and to ask what He is doing in the World today and where we ourselves are going as a species. There is then the further question as to whether this journey on which we are embarked is heading in the right direction and whether our actions are according to God's will and His present work. In this way, theology and ethics are irrevocably linked as we come to view the world through the light of God's presence and action. The things which we see with our eyes will then be transfigured as we see them afresh in a new context. Ethics and theology are interconnected through the historical narrative and this is something which we shall have to live with throughout the present work.

If we try to summarize what the distinctive Christian ethical approach to the present crisis might be, then we should start with the relationships and response which emerge from the narrative of which we are a part; a narrative which recognises both historicity and revelation. The relationships are those which we have with God, with other people and with the whole creation in its widest sense. This is more than an attitude of benevolence or a simple application of αγαπε, that distinctively Christian form of love in which we always seek the best for those about us. It is a movement which recognises the presence of failure and the idea of Sin. Immorality is not simply disobedience to a set of rules. It is a failure to do justice to the relationships of which each person is a part.

The whole of the covenant theme throughout the Old Testament and the theme of its renewal in the New Testament is about doing justice to the relationships in which we stand. This is the idea which derives from the root *sdq*, which is found in many middle-eastern languages, and which St. Paul expressed through the Greek word δικαιοσυνη (dikaiosune), usually translated into the English language as 'righteousness'. The implication is that a righteous person is one who does justice to the relationships in which he or she stands. It is important to note that this expression of relationships is spontaneous and is not about pulling ourselves up by our pelagian bootstraps. It is about being enabled by the grace of the Holy Spirit, the third person of the Divine Trinity. To be human within a relationship involves risk on both sides both because of our own failings and because of those with whom we are in relationship. This ethic is realistic, in that it acknowledges failure, but it is also hopeful, because it takes account of the faithfulness of God to those within His Covenant. Because it is an ethic set within the Christian narrative, it is an ethic which includes the cross. The cross shows the cost of overcoming the failure which occurs as we grasp at the narrative which involves going beyond what appears to be sensible. It is an ethic which avoids apportioning simplistic blame or making facile calls for the greatest overall good. An ethic which instead calls for hard choices and lives with them and their consequences as we strive, by the grace of God, to do justice to the divine image in which we are made. In essence, the distinctive element is the figure of Christ on the cross; a figure who will reappear throughout the rest of this study as we consider the interplay between the Creator, ourselves and the rest of the creation.

Notes

1. Genesis Ch.1.vv26–28. I am following the traditional source-critical account which sees Genesis Ch.1.v1 - 2.v4a and Ch.2.v4b - Ch.3 as originating from two different sources probably separated (in their written form) by several hundred years, with chapter one being the later account. The writers of this later account are usually referred to as the Priestly source, with the earlier source being termed the Yahwist. The exact timings and the manner of composition are not important in the present context.
2. Genesis Ch.3.
3. Exodus Ch.20. vv4–6.
4. A discussion of this issue can be found in the article by Moberly.
5. Dunn pp.53–73.
6. Song p.113.
7. Athanasius 'De Incarnatione' Ch.11–13.
8. Young pp.20–21.
9. Soskice (1991) p.36.
10. Barth p.330. This statement is noteworthy because of Barth's repeated emphasis on the transcendence of God and his reluctance to attach significance to the revelation of God in history.
11. Brunner pp.67f.
12. Daly (1988) pp.43–44.
13. Moltmann (1985) p.4.
14. Moltmann (1985) p.122.
15. See, 'Nature, Also, Mourns for a Lost Good' in Tillich (1949).
16. See, for instance, the account in Zahrnt, pp.325ff. This subject is also examined in chapter seven of the present work.
17. Soskice (1991) p.37.
18. White's article has come to be regarded as a classic and is frequently cited by those who seek to blame Christianity for environmental exploitation.
19. See the discussion by Arguile pp.517–519.
20. Peacocke pp.155–158 in Montefiore; Peacocke (1979) pp.276–279.
21. Hendry p.94.
22. Barbour p.17.
23. Polkinghorne (1991) pp.76f.
24. Moltmann (1985) pp.34–35.
25. Soskice (1991) p.37.
26. In chapter one of 'Religion in an Age of Science' (1990), Barbour reviews and discusses the relationship between science and religion.
27. Brunner pp.124ff.
28. Tillich op. cit.

29. Oppenheimer (1983) p.113, who cites St. Augustine's discourse on Psalm 37 v.14 from his work 'On the Psalms'.
30. Oppenheimer (1983) p.119.
31. See McFadyen (1992) p.13.
32. Montefiore pp.77f.
33. Moltmann (1985) p.5.
34. See, for example, Soskice (1991) p.35ff.
35. Daly (1988) pp.43–46.
36. Oppenheimer (1983) p.119.
37. See the essay, 'The Shaking of The Foundations', which is contained in the volume of the same title – Tillich (1949).
38. See the essay 'We believe in two orders', in Tillich (1949).
39. This distinction is expressed and explained by Tillich on pp.39ff of volume II of his Systematic Theology (1978b).
40. For a discussion of these notions of Hubris and Concupiscence, see Tillich (1978b) pp.48f.
41. Matthew Fox's work 'Original Blessing' provides an example of this approach.
42. An example of such a defence from an ecological perspective can be found in Bradley pp. 62–66.
43. Barr pp.91f.
44. See pp.99–104 of Polkinghorne (1991).
45. Hauerwas pp.24f.
46. The dilemma has its origins with Socrates who, given his culture, referred to gods rather than to one God.
47. Hauerwas p.60.
48. Tillich, pp.18–28 of volume I of his Systematic Theology (1978a).

Chapter 3

God The Creator

In chapter two it was stated that, given the present context, the most important issue in a discussion about creation is not that of how the universe was created, but rather who created it. This then leads to a consideration of what this createdness implies about the universe and about its relationship with its creator. In this chapter we shall address the nature of creation, with the intention of gaining an understanding of its creator and of His relationship with His creation.

3.1 Understanding God and Creation

In the present day, there is no simple and popular view of world origins which is universally accepted within western society. Whatever the role which biblical accounts may have played in the past, they have long since been generally ousted by scientific theories which are far too complex to provide this popular view. Books which attempt to popularise such scientific theories often sell well,[1] but it is doubtful how many of those people who buy such books actually understand the ideas which they contain. Western civilisation has therefore bred a people who do not possess an understandable and comprehensive account of their origins. Despite their apparent concern for the historical significance of important events, this is a people which has lost touch with the earliest part of its historical narrative.

Apart from those Christians who believe that the early chapters of Genesis can be understood as literal truth, the same lack of contact with our origins is also true for those within The Christian Church. We often feel that we should be looking to these creation narratives, but we are sceptical of doing so because of our awareness of developments in scientific understanding. We need to rediscover not only the meaning of these accounts, but also the nature of the relationships which result if we accept the doctrine of the Creator God.

The creation narratives contained in the early chapters of Genesis seem to have been produced as a synthesis of the extant knowledge of the known world and, in particular, to parallel and yet contrast with similar accounts from other ancient near-eastern cultures. This is particularly noticeable in the Priestly account of chapter one, which sees creation as being a deliberate action by God rather than being the by-product of a deitific battle as is the case with the Babylonian and Ugaritic accounts.[2] This particular account also describes creation from nothing (*ex nihilo*) rather than from pre-existent material. God is understood not merely as some entity who makes things from what He finds lying around, but as the truly creative God who brings into being all that has been, is and will be. This view also implies that the world is separate from God,[3] although we should note that this issue is often contested (see below).

The context in which the biblical creation narratives are set is also of particular importance. The people of Israel had experienced their God, Yahweh, as the God of History, and were attempting to discover both their own origins and the origins of their relationship with this God. They were attempting to locate their present human experience in a framework of larger significance. This quest reached its fullest expression at a time of crisis, namely the time of the Babylonian exile. Their description of the Creator God is therefore found not only in the final formulation of Genesis Ch.1-11, but also in writings such as Isaiah Ch.40-55 and certain of the psalms where Yahweh the Creator God is linked to His saving action within history.[4] This is not to claim that creation was not already a theme in the life of this people, but to emphasise that their understanding of creation stressed a dependence on God and a response of wonder and affirmation of the world. In the present crisis we again need to find such historic links to the roots of our faith and to be open to perceive the creative action of God in the world.

The South-American Liberation theologian Gustavo Gutierrez has claimed that the purpose of the biblical creation narratives is not so much to provide an account of World origins, as to form a starting point for Salvation-History. Creation is therefore seen as the opening up of the historical perspective, with the initiation of history and what he describes as the 'Salvific Adventure'.[5] Creation is the beginning of the narrative of which we are now a part and an affirmation that God is involved in the universe. However, we should be careful to observe that ancient Israel did not see history and nature in the same way as we do today. The concept of continuous natural laws was alien to her, and she was more ready to see the work of God in the events of daily life than is often the case at the present time.[6] This world-view can be seen on the one hand as an openness to the work of God, but on the other hand as an approach akin to that of 'God of the gaps', in which God is invoked to fill-in for every gap in human understanding until that gap can be filled by other means. Such gaps are, of course, often used erroneously as evidence for the existence of God.

If we examine the place which man was thought to occupy in this world-view, then in chapter two of Genesis we discover the clear statement that man has the same origin as other creatures but that he is granted power over them. This power is demonstrated by man being given the authority to name his fellow creatures – knowledge of names and especially the authority to grant names was understood as conveying power over that for which the name was known. All power is, of course, relative and in this case it is restricted by the fact that man is himself a part of creation. This perception is demonstrated by Psalm 104, which may well contain an earlier account of creation than Genesis chapter two.[7] Here, we find little if any difference in status between man and his fellow creatures. The superiority of man was not so prominent in the earliest accounts.

By the time of the writing of the Priestly account in the first chapter of Genesis, the perceived status of man had changed. The human creature was now made in the image and likeness

of God, with the Hebrew implying that this was a deep correspondence and not related only to appearance or to spirit and
intellect.[8] Moreover, at the point when God created man
(Genesis Ch.1 v27) the Hebrew word used is *bara'*, the word
reserved for divine creation from nothing, *ex nihilo*, as in v1
when the heavens and the earth are formed. The creation of all
other creatures is described using the word *asah*, as they are
brought forth from the earth or 'made', so that man is clearly
seen as a distinct form of life. He is distanced from nature, a
theme which recurs in Psalm 8. It is important to note in this
context that the word *bara'* has no human analogy and conveys
the idea of the production of something entirely novel, without
the use of pre-existent material. As Moltmann has observed,
this implies that the world is produced entirely by the will of
God, but is separate from God.[9] The Israelite creation tradition stressed the fact that the world was created in this way and
was not simply an emanation of God as was the case in the
nature religions with which they were in contact.[10]

This distinction is to be understood as placing man in the
position of an ideal king who should care for creation. Man
becomes the mediator between God and Nature and is
expected to live in perfect obedience to God.[11] This is the
picture stressed in neo-orthodoxy, the twentieth century theological movement typified by the work of Karl Barth, which
sees the opening chapters of Genesis as symbolising the basic
relationship between humanity, the world and God, including
human creatureliness.[12] In reading the biblical creation narrative, chapter one is too often taken in isolation from what
follows. If the Priestly account is followed through the
succeeding chapters, we discover that man becomes corrupt in
the sight of God and that the consequence of this corruption is
the flood.

In attempts to demonstrate the goodness of nature and to
justify the place of ecology within Christianity, stress is often
laid on the word 'good' which God uses to describe His
creation in Genesis chapter one. Writers who use this argument usually fail to explain why God went on to destroy this
'good' creation in the flood, long before humanity had the
chance to cause widespread environmental damage. In fact, as
James Barr has observed, the prologues to the accounts of the

flood in chapter six of Genesis inform us of the wickedness which was present on the earth and of God's determination to put an end to it.[13] The relevant prologues include the Priestly version which comes from the same source as the account of the creation which is recorded in chapter one and in which the creation is described as being 'good'.

After the flood the Priestly sources contain a treaty or covenant between God and every living creature and indeed with the Earth itself.[14] Here, man is placed in equality with all other creatures. Yet in the preceding verses the actual state which exists is also shown, with God telling Noah that every living creature will live in fear and dread of him.[15] In this narrative there would therefore appear to be both a statement of the ideal situation and a recognition of the reality which actually exists. God states His purposes that the earth will never again be destroyed by such a flood and yet the reality of human failing is all too apparent.

The ancient people of Israel developed the above ideas to explain the world in the context of their daily relationship with Yahweh. Today, we no longer have to invoke the action of God to explain the various facets of human existence, since we have scientific explanations for most of what we experience. Taken to its natural conclusion this situation has resulted in a state of mind which often refuses to allow God any role in the events which occur in the world. There is a confusion between descriptions of the way in which the world works and an explanation of why the world is as it is. Many people now believe that science will eventually be able to explain everything, if not now then at some time in the future. Within popular thought, the limitations of scientific prediction are either unrealised or unknown.

The idea of a God who acts in and through human history is often rejected and the popular conception is of a God who has to justify his existence, especially in the light of suffering and evil in the world. Such a view of God is not new and was probably on the mind of the author(s) of the book of Job. Indeed, at around the same time that Job was written, the Greek philosopher Epicurus asked: 'Is God willing to prevent evil, but not able? Then he is impotent. Is he able but not willing? Then he is malevolent. Is he both able and willing?

Whence this evil?' Despite these historical roots such views of God are now accepted in ways which would not have been possible in earlier times and God is often portrayed as a human construct, or as being 'non-real'.[16] Such a God has important and significant similarities with the way in which God is described in Scholastic theology, in that He is both distant from the world and unmoved by His creation. As Gabriel Daly notes, the God of Scholastic Theology has to be unmoved because to move is to change and God cannot change because He is perfect.[17]

Yet despite the similarities, the Scholastic theologians had an uncritical belief in a realist God and also accepted the traditional views of world origins which we do not accept today. It is perhaps the triumph of their ideas and their perpetuation into our own time which has led to the present lack of confidence in God and the lack of understanding of the scientific-theological dialogue in popular thought. Scholastic theology could not cope with the rise of scientific thinking in the nineteenth century and became a closed system of thought impervious to any outside influence. The works of Catholic Modernist writers such as Alfred Loisy and George Tyrrell, who attempted to bridge the gap as well as to consider divine immanence, were condemned in Papal Decrees and placed on the index of prohibited books.

The idea of a separation between God and creation has more recently been reinforced by two strands of twentieth century theology. Neo-orthodoxy has emphasised the transcendence of God over the world, with divine interaction occurring outside the normal history of world events (which are referred to as 'historie') and through specific ahistorical occurrence (geschichte). By way of a contrast, in existential theology, the emphasis has been on the interior nature of religion and its impact on the individual. In both cases God is again understood as being separate from nature. This separation becomes even more extreme in those theologies which postulate a non-realist God, as this precludes any possibility whatsoever of the divine making contact with the natural world. The transcendence of God over and beyond His creation is stressed to the extent that any account of His immanence to that creation is lost.

3.2 God's Closeness to Creation

The developments described in the previous section led to God being seen as remote and unaffected by the world, and yet they have also led to Him being blamed for not intervening to prevent human illness and death. Such a god would be a god who meddles from afar and who has no local knowledge or understanding. As John Macquarrie has noted, this asymmetrical monarchical vision is produced by a world which has need of God, but which cannot conceive that God could possibly be interested in the world.[18] It is a further expression of the notion of a dominant, unitarian and patriarchal God, a notion which envisages a highly asymmetric relationship between God and man. In this expression it is very easy to understand how and why human suffering can occur and very difficult to reconcile such suffering with the concept of a God who is described as love. In such a scheme, theodicy is almost inevitably expressed through the often repeated statement that either God does not care or that he is dead.[19] We are drawn to ask how a God who is remote can be described as love and how a God who is described as love can allow suffering? If God is indeed perfect, as Scholastic Theologians have claimed, is it not possible that such perfection might imply a love which can understand the suffering of His creation?

These questions have direct implications for the current environmental crisis. If we believe that man is damaging the creation, then the vision of a remote and transcendent God outlined above leads to the same conclusions. God is either unable to act because He is dead, or is He unwilling to act because He no longer cares for His creation.

Such a scenario is unacceptable within the Christian faith. It is unacceptable not only because it ignores God's statement that creation is 'good' and His promise never to harm it again after the flood, but also because it does not take account of the Christian belief that God affirmed the potential goodness within his creation through the incarnation. In the incarnation we are called to accept that Jesus Christ has revealed the sacramental nature of the world.[20] Despite our persistent anthropocentrism, we need to recognise that all living creatures are composed of the same matter, whilst also believing that in man this same matter was able to express the person-hood of God. A modern view of the incarnation might be, that in the human species the evolutionary process has resulted in a creature which in religious terms can be the instrument for the expression of the presence of God in the world, and which in scientific terms is aware of its own presence and of its failure to care for the world.

A way forward from this vision of a transcendent and distant God was suggested during the late nineteenth and early twenti-eth centuries by the catholic modernist theologian George Tyrrell. Tyrrell coined the term 'panentheism' to refer to God as being present in and caring for all things in themselves, as well as being transcendent to them.[21] In so doing he made the important point that the transcendence and the immanence of God are closely related.

A number of modern theologians have combined this concept of panentheism with the philosophical school of Process Thought in an attempt to hold together the ideas of God as transcendent and immanent. In his examination of God in a nuclear context, Jim Garrison notes that just because we do not find God when we look for Him or just because He does not intervene at a time of crisis, does not necessarily imply that He is dead. The alternative conclusion to draw is that we have been looking for Him in the wrong way, or that we have a faulty view of God. He sees Process Theology as providing the insights needed for us to make a more successful search as well as enabling us to cope with the problem of evil, whilst still being true to biblical traditions which are an inte-gral part of the Christian faith.[22]

Process Theology finds its origins in the thought of the English philosopher and mathematician Alfred North Whitehead, who suggested that all things are interconnected and that there is no true individual existence. As a result, exis-tence is not a fixed state or being, rather it is a process of realisation or becoming. In this way, the universe continually moves forward, or evolves, towards new expressions or 'actual entities' all of which are inter-related. For Whitehead, God is the chief exemplification of this scheme as well as being the one eternal entity which makes it all possible. God is the ground of order, the ground of novelty and is influenced by the world. However, within this scheme all things are interrelated and so God too has to exist in a related state. As a result, God is not before creation but with creation. According to Whitehead, it is God who places the purpose and possibility within each temporal event; not as a remote monarchical God, but as a God who is actually present.[23]

However, Whitehead's theology would appear to devalue the divine nature of God in an effort to avoid a remote transcendence. Although it points to the doctrine of God as Creator, it appears to deny God the opportunity to create, since all creation is concomitant with God. The North-American Process Philosopher Charles Hartshorne wanted to stress both sides of God, and did so through the idea of a dual transcendence in which God is both 'primordial' or independent of creation, as well as being 'consequent' or dependent on creation. The result of his arguments was that since God is therefore dependent on His creation, it becomes meaningful to speak of God as evolving. This idea is summarised in Hartshorne's statement: 'God is a being whose versatility of becoming is unlimited'.[24] God is therefore seen as being both within us and beyond us, and the universe progresses through a loving interaction between the Creator and His creation in which He will not let further creation cease. This scheme allows both the physical expression of God and His indwelling within creation since that creation is a part of Him.

Garrison defines panentheism as a state in which God is everywhere, with nothing outside Him, but in which the totality of all things is less than God. As a literal translation demonstrates, everything is in God. This understanding carries the implication that if God contains the Universe then He is affected by activity within the Universe and is thereby vulnerable.[25] Daly notes that such Process Thought is useful in its correction of the monarchical view of God, and in the way in which it holds God's passibility and impassibility together.[26] This is the concept which Macquarrie termed 'dialectical theism', in which the transcendent God consents to know and share in pain and frustration, by creating a world in which such things are inevitably present.[27] Within this scheme, human disregard for the environment can be seen not only as damage to God's creation, but also as an attack upon God

Himself. It results in a clear Christian imperative to care for the environment.

3.3 Some Problems with An Immanent God

There are three major problems with the approaches to the doctrine of an immanent God outlined in section 3.2, and with the conclusions which are drawn by Garrison. The first problem is that this approach is supposed to introduce to theology the idea of God as 'becoming' rather than as being fixed in His nature. However, there is nothing new in this idea of God as 'becoming', because it is precisely the way in which He revealed Himself to the people of ancient Israel.

When God revealed His name to Moses in Exodus Ch.3 v14, this name was understood as a revelation of His nature. A name expressed the nature of the person or object who bore that name. However, the name which God revealed to Moses, namely 'YHWH', contains a multiple ambiguity concerning the part of speech to which it belongs. This ambiguity is perhaps intentional, in that the name of God should not be wholly known or understood. This tenseless Hebrew form conveys not only the idea that 'I am what I am', which is the most common translation of 'YHWH', but also that 'I will be what I will be' and 'I will become what I will become'.[28] Moreover, the Hebrew is not an abstract statement of being from a remote deity, but rather a statement of concern from a God who is with His people. It is as if God is saying 'I will be what I will be on your behalf'. Through His self-revelation to Moses, God is already dynamic in the way in which His name is recorded in the Hebrew Scriptures.[29] Through the disclosure of His name, God expressed His unlimited capacity of becoming some three and a half thousand years before the development of Process Theology.

The second problem concerns Whitehead's claim that because Process Theology tells us that God has to exist in a related state, then He cannot have been before creation but rather had to be with creation in order that He could relate to something. In making this claim Whitehead misses the insight which is provided by the doctrine of the Trinity, namely that there is a relatedness within the Godhead. Furthermore, this idea of relatedness predates the full development of the doctrine of The Trinity because both New Testament and early patristic writers described the Word of God as being eternally present with the Father and the earlier Hebrew writers described Wisdom as God's creative agent. Both of these descriptions imply a relatedness in God without the creation being present.

Hartshorne also appears to have reinvented patristic expressions for God within his discussion. When he wrote about 'primordial' and 'consequent' God he was using ideas very similar to the concepts of λογοσ ενδιαθετοσ (logos endiathetos) and λογοσ σπερματικοσ (logos spermatikos) which were used by early Christian apologists such as Justin Martyr who borrowed them from Greek philosophy. λογοσ ενδιαθετοσ expressed the presence of The Word of God with the Father and λογοσ σπερματικοσ the immanence of The Word of God in the world. In this description, God's immanence and His transcendence are closely related. Whether or not we now accept these ideas from the patristic period as being a valid description of God, they do express the very concepts which Hartshorne claimed could be contributed by Process Theology. They provide a description of God in His creation as well as allowing for relationship to exist within the Godhead.

The third problem with this approach occurs in Garrison's discussion of evil, and in what he describes as the darkness of the post-Hiroshima age. Garrison sees God as creating natural evil, and therefore sees God's handiwork in the bombing of Hiroshima. Rather than being totally good, Garrison sees God as having a 'dark side' to His nature, although he does move on to note that God creatively integrates all aspects of reality, both good and evil, to produce an overall benevolence.[30] In support of his argument he quotes the Cyrus oracle from Isaiah Ch.45 and in particular verse seven in which God creates (*bara'*) darkness and woe. This is the only biblical instance of such a statement in which the creation of evil, darkness and woe are attributed to God. The question is whether the prophet was intending this as an absolute statement, as Garrison seems to believe, or whether, as Westermann suggests, it is hyperbole to stress the creative power of the God of Iśrael whose divinity extends far beyond the limitations of human thought.[31] Westermann's suggestion is supported by the fact that the statement stands in contrast to other accounts of creation in which the emphasis is placed on God separating light from darkness and on His overcoming chaos.

Garrison's dialectical theism also seems to contain a circular argument. His notion that God created pain in order to experience pain begs the question as to why He needed to know pain in the first place. The only reason why God should want or need to know pain is in order to share the experience of His creation. However, if He had not created the pain then the need would not have arisen. The belief that evil originated with God also poses a moral problem since it makes it difficult to distinguish between good and evil. In order to make such a distinction we have to set ourselves up in judgement on God and decide which is which rather than finding guidance from God.

The theological problem which we produce by supposing that evil originates as a deliberate or accidental act of God has been recognised by authors such as Grace Jantzen.[32] Jantzen has applied panentheistic ideas to the modern world and produced a theology in which she sees the universe and God as co-existent. She argues from the premise that if God's creation of the universe was not an arbitrary action, but rather an intrinsic part of His nature – God is inherently creative – then the universe and God have always been co-existent, for to claim otherwise is to specify an arbitrary time for creation. Indeed, Jantzen claims that the universe should be seen as being formed from God's being and energy, rather than from nothing. As such, the universe can be regarded as the body of God and as his physical presence.[33] Jantzen is quick to observe that this does not imply that this particular form of the universe has always existed, only that some form has always been manifest as an expression of God's being.[34]

Jantzen's concept of the world as God's body can be related to the Gaia hypothesis of Lovelock, in which he sees the whole of the earth and all living things as constituting a single entity which has a power beyond their individual capabilities. He terms this entity Gaia.[35] Gaia is able to control the composition of its own atmosphere and its global temperature through the use of a range of feedback mechanisms, although it should be noted that there is no implication in Lovelock's writings that Gaia is in any sense purposeful or sentient. In this context, it is notable that when the eighteenth century Scottish philosopher and historian David Hume refuted the teleological argument for the existence of God (the argument from design), he did so on the grounds that the world much more resembled a living organism than an artifact.

It is important to note that Gaia is an hypothesis, not a discovery of fact as sometimes appears to be claimed in the arguments which are put forward by the supporters of Lovelock. Indeed, it can be argued that it is not even a scientific hypothesis because its verification or refutation lies beyond the abilities of scientific methods. In many ways Gaia has become an alternative faith rather than an hypothesis which can be tested, and one which has fundamental tenets which are inimicable to Christianity. One such belief is the view that Gaia will act in such a way as to rid itself of anything which poses a threat to its continued existence. In the present context this would imply the eradication of the human species irrespective of our lifestyle. This is a conclusion which stands in stark contrast to the Christian doctrine of the atonement. The theological implications of the Gaia hypothesis have been discussed in more detail by Celia Deane-Drummond.[36]

Although Jantzen concedes that God's apparent creation of evil in her theory constitutes a problem, she sees it as presenting no more of a problem than the presence of evil in a theology of creation *ex nihilo*. She explains evil by the common argument that the perfect love of God allows freedom of action in His creation.[37] Daly agrees that this approach presents the best explanation which we can devise in order to explain pain and suffering in the world. He echoes the traditional view that the ultimate hope rests in an eschatological future.[38] However, Daly is also at pains to point out that although this argument is satisfactory when stated in abstract terms, its theodicy does not work in practice. The hope of an eschatological future is not a sufficient answer to the human perception of present sufferings and there can be no cheap or superficial answers to such problems.[39] Daly repeats the view of Dostoyevski, placed on the lips of Ivan Karamazov, that no explanation can justify sufferings which have to be endured by children.[40] In the same way it can be contended that belief in and hope for an eschatological future cannot be used to justify human actions and attitudes which are damaging to the environment, even if ultimately, such an eschatological future is the divine response to evil. If eschatological theology is inadequate as a solace for our own human sufferings, then we should not use it to justify or to atone for our damage to the environment.

In addressing the questions of evil, it is both more helpful and pertinent to respond by stating God's acceptance of responsibility for the failings of the world. This is not to agree that God created evil, either purposefully or accidentally, nor is it an attempt to apportion blame, rather it is a statement of hope based upon the reality of the cross. In Jesus Christ we can see God taking the negative possibilities and evil in the world into Himself. As the writer of the Epistle to the Colossians observed, these are nailed to the cross in the same way as are the bond which stood against us and its legal demands (Colossians Ch.2 v14). Whatever pain and suffering occur in the world, God accepts the consequences in Himself irrespective of their cause.

The arguments which Jantzen uses reveal the weaknesses which are present within the whole construct which is provided by panentheism. Her argument that a universe has always existed, because to claim otherwise implies an arbitrariness in the creative nature of God, misses a key aspect of the nature of creation. If God created time and matter together, *ex nihilo,* then to speak of a time before creation (when creation did not exist) is completely meaningless. This co-creation of time and matter is not only supported by relativity theory, which sees time as a fourth dimension, but also by theological and philosophical thought.[41] In writing of the actions of God before creation, Augustine noted: 'Let them see that there could be no time without a created being and let them cease to speak that vanity'.[42] Macquarrie notes that we cannot imagine creation without time or time without creation, and goes on to argue that theology cannot tell us about the time when the cosmic process began, nor to answer the question as to whether it has always existed.[43] In his writing on what happened before the Big Bang, the physicist Paul Davies notes 'Cause and effect are temporal concepts, and cannot be applied to a state in which time does not exist; the question is meaningless'.[44] Even if creativity is an intrinsic part of divine being, there can be no causal necessity for creation in the absence of time. God cannot be accused of creating at an arbitrary time if time did not exist.

However, supporters of panentheism tend to reject the arguments outlined above. Jantzen posits that 'If any reason for creation can be given, why was that reason not eternally sufficient?'[45] The present contention is that the reason has eternal sufficiency (i.e. it is valid both within time and outside time), but that it is meaningless to talk of a time prior to creation, and as such it is meaningless to talk of God creating at an arbitrary moment. Moments do not exist in the absence of time. We should also notice that such arguments seem to imply that existence is an attribute which is given to something by God as part of His creative action. However, the ontological proofs for the existence of God are usually refuted on the grounds that existence is not a predicate; that existence is not an attribute which is to be ascribed to an object. If this is the case, then we have to question the validity of questioning why the reason for creation was not eternally sufficient. It may be that the faults in Jantzen's thesis are essentially two aspects of the same problem, namely that existence as we know it only makes sense within time and that to discuss existence in the absence of time is meaningless. Just as distances do not exist in the absence of space, so moments do not exist in the absence of time.

In a faith which is a historical faith, an understanding of time is important, but modern scientific explanations and understandings are beyond the reach of most people. This problem is all the more pronounced if we hope to discuss events which occurred in the beginning of time, or if we want to examine matters from an eschatological perspective. The relationship between time and theology and the way in which the latter has misunderstood the former has been explored by MacKenzie.[46]

Moltmann commenting on the conclusion from Process Thought that God creates order from chaos rather than matter from nothing, noted that such creation would be described as *'asah* rather than the biblical term of *bara'*.[47] Indeed, to reject the concept of creation *ex nihilo* would be to deny one of the major insights of the Hebrew accounts of creation, an insight which distinguished them from the beliefs of the neighbouring nations. However, what is more revealing about creation and panentheism is Jantzen's argument that this particular version of the Universe need not always have existed, only that some particular form need have done so.[48] This statement clearly implies that there is an arbitrariness on the part of God about the time at which this particular universe was formed, and indeed that there is an arbitrariness about whether it should be formed at all. As a result, Jantzen's particular expression of panentheism is demonstrably associated with an arbitrariness in the divine creation, in stark contrast to the claim that panentheism removes the possibility of arbitrariness in the creative activity of God.

The former Bishop of South Carolina, C. FitzSimons Allison, has attacked what he sees as the casualness with which the teachings of theologians such as Grace Jantzen, Matthew Fox and Sallie McFague are being received and accepted by the Church. In removing the distinction between The Creator and his creation, they are claiming for nature those attributes which the Church has historically reserved for Jesus Christ. In so doing they are robbing the Church of a personal God to which it and its members can relate.[49]

We need to accept that there is a difference between the uncreated God and the created Universe. If we see the World as being part of God, then not only do we lose the personal God and diminish Christ, but we also lose an insight and understanding which the Israelites grasped many centuries before Christ. This insight is expressed in the belief that the Universe did not have to be created, but was contingent upon the love of God. In considering the contingency which exists in creation, Stephen Platten notes that, 'The creation of the Universe was a spontaneous act of divine love.'[50] This contingency of the creation (which we should contrast to the non-contingency of God as Necessary Being) demonstrates the truth of the notion that creation is neither divine nor is it God's body, albeit that He indwells His creation in the Holy Spirit.

The distinction is that unlike pantheism and panentheism, God The Holy Spirit indwells the world without the world being God or a part of God.

It is the above contingency which is the source of the Human Freedom which we take so much for granted. Although, as Platten notes, this freedom is tied up with failure and sin[51], it is also linked to our responsibility to work with God. If we had no freedom then we could have no responsibility. Our very freedom is the challenge to work for divine purposes, a challenge which must surely include the caring for the creation. This is what Moltmann has expressed when he sees us standing before God on behalf of creation and before creation on behalf of God.[52]

3.4 Understanding The Creator Today

The arguments outlined above are not presented in order to deny that there may be lessons that can be learnt or understandings which can be drawn from Process Theology, but rather to cast doubt on the idea that it has a place in the process of reconciling Christian thought with the modern world. In fact, the insights into the divine which Process Theology and Panentheism are claimed to provide are already present within the traditional Christian doctrines of The Incarnation and God the Holy Trinity. In these doctrines the physical expression of God in his creation is provided by The Son, although to say this is not to claim that God is not also revealed through His creation. Indeed, the second person of the Trinity can be seen as the first expression of otherness. The Word of God can be seen as both the creative agent and the first born of creation – both the differentiation within God and the expression of that differentiation. Again, this is what early Christian apologists would have referred to as λογοσ ενδιαθετοσ and λογοσ σπερματικοσ.

This theme was later taken up in the third century by Origen who explored the consequences of eternal differentiation in the Godhead.[53] For Origen, Christ was begotten before all things and all things were made through Him. Crucially, Origen recognised that because the Father is outside time and because

He is eternally the Father, then the Son must be outside time too and therefore also be eternal.[54] This argument is not entirely satisfactory, for Origen was later condemned as a heretic partly on the charge that he applied similar arguments in deducing that if God is eternally creative then there must have been eternal creation. Origen apparently failed to notice that there is a difference between the Son and creation. This difference relies on the fact that the concept of existence can only make sense within time and that outside time its descriptive powers break down. Since the Son is divine then it makes sense to speak of Him as eternally 'being' with the Father. Because creation is not divine then the same arguments do not apply.

In the fourth century, Athanasius, the bishop of Alexandria, worked hard to defend the doctrine of The Incarnation against heresies which denied either the true divinity of Christ or His true humanity. In doing so he came to understand the Word of God as containing all things in Himself, and yet at the same time as being outside all things and sustaining the life of the universe. Athanasius' understanding of The Incarnation is explained in his work 'De Incarnatione Verbi Dei' from which the following extract is taken.[55]

'The Word was not hedged in by His body, nor did His presence in the body prevent His being elsewhere as well. When He moved His body He did not cease to direct the universe by His Mind and might. The marvellous truth is, that being the Word, so far from being Himself contained by anything, He actually contained all things Himself. In creation He is present everywhere, yet is distinct in being from it; ordering, directing, giving life to all, containing all, yet is He Himself the Uncontained, existing solely in His Father. As with the whole, so also is it with the part. Existing in a human body, to which He Himself gives life, He is still Source of life to all the universe, present in every part of it, yet outside the whole...'

These Greek expressions of Christian teaching had earlier parallels in the Hebrew wisdom literature. Here, Wisdom is before creation and is also the first of the works of God

(Proverbs, Ch.8 vv22ff). Creation therefore includes the creation of relationships, rather than only being concerned with material objects and individuals. We shall see in chapter five that it can be argued that for a relationship to be fully realised then there needs to be a third person who exists outside the relationship and enables the distinction to be made between relationship and non-relationship. Within Christian teaching this condition is satisfied within the Godhead through the understanding of God as Trinity.

These important Christian doctrines help to correct the distorted image of a god who is wholly transcendent and distant, and help to draw our image of the divine back into contact with the immanent creation. The insights and corrections which panentheism is supposed to provide are only necessary because the implications of the doctrine of the Trinity have frequently been ignored. Too often, we equate the word 'God' with a patriarchal image of 'God the Father' with the result that the second and third persons of the Trinity are neglected or even ignored entirely.

Moltmann notes the distortion by which God is seen as a monotheistic and absolute subject. He writes:

'If we cease to understand God monotheistically as the one, absolute subject, but instead see him in a trinitarian sense as the unity of the Father, the Son and the Spirit, we can then no longer, either, conceive his relationship to the world he has created as a one-sided relationship of domination'.[56]

He goes on to note that creation is by the Father, through the Son and in the Holy Spirit: that God creates other; that God reconciles and redeems other; and that God dwells in and experiences other.[57] Indeed, we should note that the concept of the Holy Spirit indwelling creaturely beings bears a close resemblance to the panentheistic God who encompasses the whole creation. Perhaps the development of panentheism as an allegedly Christian teaching amounts to no more than a rediscovery of The Holy Spirit.

However, both the transcendence and the immanence of God can be misunderstood in themselves and they are much more closely related than is often realised to be the case. John Barton, Professor of The Interpretation of Holy Scripture at Oxford University, has noted that for Jews and Christians to speak of God's transcendence is not to speak of remoteness but rather of grace.[58] The transcendence of God does not signify a god who is remote and uninterested in us, but rather The God who cannot be confined by our ideas about Him. God's transcendence and His otherness is actually good news because a god who was just like us would be no god.

Barton believes that God's immanence has similarly been misconstrued. A god who is near to us can be thought of as a god whom we can control, a sort of cuddly pet god. God's presence with us is not only a comfort, but also a demand, because we cannot escape from Him and from His presence. We cannot hide from Him and all our actions our open to Him whether we like it or not. The immanent God is not a cosy god just as the transcendent God is not a remote god. God will be what He will be, but He will be it in His concern for His creation.

In his discussion of immanence and transcendence, Ross Thompson, a Church of England priest, notes that God's transcendence and immanence are inter-dependent. In order to sustain the World, God must be both other than the World (an external agent) and also within the World, for if He were not the latter then He would be unable to act. 'As source of being, he is other; as activity of being, he is ever present.'[59] Thompson goes on to note: 'Immanence opens up an epistemological transcendence that makes God more 'wholly other' than anything in Karl Barth!' The immanence and the transcendence of God are not simply two ideas to be used when required or even to be held together in tension. They contribute, rely on and inform each other. There is a co-inherence about them such that the one is not possible without the other.

In attempting to maintain human responsibility in the created order but without anthropocentrism, Stephen Platten has made use of the views of Gregory of Nyssa. For Gregory, humanity is placed in an independent Universe, and the Universe and God relate via co-inherence or perichoresis.[60] Co-inherence refers to God's participation in the world and the world's participation in God, but without identifying God with the creation. In such a scheme of things, the alleviation of environmental problems in the world would be achieved through a responsible human cooperation with God.

Although Process Theology and Panentheism have been successful in providing a theological understanding of change and especially of evolution, any rejection of these schools of thought does not necessarily preclude such theological understanding. Evolution is too often seen as deterministic and operating within the fixed laws of a mechanical universe which could have been set in motion by a remote transcendent god. In reality, our understanding of molecular biology shows us that evolution relies on random changes in genetic material. Such changes are by no means always for the better and certain uncorrected changes of this type are one cause of cancer. Essentially, what we are doing when we think in this way is to apply the same freedom which we associated with a loving God in the context of human evil, to the love of God as expressed in the context of molecular processes. The same freedom which gives the potential for love, growth and development at all levels, is also the freedom which allows disease and decay. This is the theme of entropy again. A local negative change in entropy (a decrease in disorder) is necessary for life, but a positive change is necessary for the new possibilities which are inherent in growth and evolution. However, this positive change carries with it the risk of other changes which are damaging to the whole. We can use this idea to apply a modern interpretation to verses 18-25 of the eighth chapter of Paul's letter to the Romans. Here, we read that the way to the redemption of humanity from evil has been made known in Jesus Christ, whilst the rest of the created order still awaits its redemption from the negative possibilities which it experiences.

A possible way of expressing these ideas in more familiar language, is through the concept of play. We shall examine play in more detail in chapters seven and eight, but it is worth noting here that real play is both a free and spontaneous activity and a chain of actions with both system and purpose. This definition matches the way in which we have been discussing creation. Play enables humanity to cope with the contingency and chance in the world: the contingency which is present within creation. Moltmann has noted the importance of Play as a symbol[61] and Hugo Rahner writes in a way which refutes the panentheistic argument of a necessary creation, when he notes that the concept of play implies that creation 'though a divinely meaningful act, was by no means a necessary one, as far as God Himself was concerned.'[62] If this is correct then neither should creation be described as being utilitarian. Creation is rather a joyful and spontaneous action, the results of which delighted and continue to delight their creator. We shall return to this important theme in chapter eight, where we shall examine its implications for the Church.

The way forward to understanding redemption, or God's conquest of sin, evil and negativity, lies in accepting the idea that creation is a continual activity of God, rather than a one-off action which occurred only once at the beginning of time. The creative God is continually active to overcome or negate the negative possibilities in the world. We have already noted the occurrence of the word *bara'* throughout the Old Testament, and comparable references to new creation occur in the New Testament.[63] The creation and salvation which are wrought by God can both be seen as parts of one ongoing process and it is to this idea that we shall now turn.

Notes

1. A good example of such a book is 'A Brief History of Time', by Stephen Hawking.
2. For a good discussion of creation narratives from different cultures, see 'God's Conflict with the Dragon and the Sea', by John Day.
3. Young p.30.
4. Specific examples include Psalms 74 and 89 together with Isaiah Ch. 43 vv18–19; Ch. 48 and Ch. 51 v9–16.
5. Gutierrez pp.153f. See also Von Rad (1975) pp.139f and (1965) p.341.
6. Discussed by Von Rad (1965) pp.336ff.
7. See, for instance, the account in Weiser pp.633ff.
8. Von Rad (1975) pp.144–145.
9. Moltmann (1985) pp.72ff.
10. See Von Rad (1965) pp.338ff.
11. Baker pp.92ff. in Montefiore.
12. Barbour pp.11–12.

13. See Barr pp.74ff.
14. Genesis Ch.9 vv10,12,15,16,17 and v13. respectively. According to Bernhard Anderson's appendix to Noth, these verses are all from the Priestly author.
15. Genesis Ch.9 vv1–9. See Baker pp.94ff. in Montefiore.
16. Writers such as Ludwig Feuerbach, Friedrich Neitzsche and Don Cupitt have explored and promoted the idea that God is a product of human conciousness.
17. Daly (1988) p.18. See also Daly (1980).
18. See Macquarrie (1975) pp.111ff.
19. These conclusions are by no means new, but they are implied for the present context by Daly (1988) p.26.
20. Peacocke pp.137ff in Montefiore.
21. Tyrrell pp.250ff; see also Daly (1988) pp.35ff.
22. Garrison pp.15ff.
23. Garrison pp.29f; Whitehead pp.584ff.
24. Hartshorne p.6, quoted by Garrison.
25. Garrison pp.44ff.
26. Daly (1988) pp.23ff.
27. Daly (1988) p.24; Macquarrie (1984) p.180.
28. See Von Rad (1975) pp.179ff.
29. A discussion of the verb form and its meanings can be found in Johnstone (1990).
30. Garrison discusses this on pp.21ff.
31. Westermann (1969) pp.161f.
32. See p.136 of Jantzen (1984).
33. Jantzen (1984) p.143.
34. Jantzen (1984) pp.131ff.
35. Lovelock (1979) and (1988).
36. Deane–Drummond (1992). It is important to recognise that unlike Christian Theology, the Gaia hypothesis contains no moral imperative for the preservation either of the human race or of any other species.
37. Jantzen (1984) p.152.
38. Daly (1988) pp.25ff.
39. Daly (1988) pp.148ff.
40. Dostoyevski p.287.
41. Einstein's General Theory of Relativity is actually neutral on the issue of whether or not the universe was created. The point which is being made here is that within this theory time is simply another dimension alongside the three dimensions of space. As a result it is meaningless to talk of time already being present when the physicality of the universe came into being.
42. Augustine 'Confessions' *11*.30.

43. Macquarrie (1977) pp.216f.
44. Davies p.39.
45. Jantzen (1984) p.139.
46. MacKenzie (1993).
47. Moltmann (1985) pp.78f.
48. Jantzen (1984) p.141.
49. Allison (1994) pp.165ff.
50. Platten (1991) p.23.
51. Platten (1991) pp.25–26.
52. Moltmann (1985) p.190.
53. Origen, De Principiis, I.2.10.
54. Origen, De Pricipiis, I.2.4.
55. The extract is from chapter seventeen with the translation being that of the Mowbray edition of 1953.
56. Moltmann (1985) p.2.
57. Moltmann (1985) p.9,15.
58. Barton (1996) pp.55f.
59. See R. Thompson pp.23ff.
60. Platten (1991) p.27.
61. Moltmann (1985) p.310.
62. H. Rahner (1967) p.11.
63. The idea of new creation in the New Testament is found in II Corinthians Ch.5 v17. The Cosmic Christ of Col Ch.1 vv15–20 and I Corinthians Ch.8 v6 also carries this implication.

Chapter 4

God The Saviour

We have now established something of the nature of the Creation, its relationship with its Creator and the threats which face it. These threats need to be considered in the context of the Judaeo-Christian belief that God is faithful not only to Himself and to who He is, but also to all His people and to that which He has made. This faithfulness of God then raises the question as to the nature of the divine response to the creation which is under threat. What is the gospel, or 'Good News' for a damaged world and how is creation to be redeemed?

As we have already suggested, the answer to the questions surrounding redemption lie within the notion of a continually creative God and the way in which this creativity is related to the saving action of the second person of the Trinity. The death and resurrection of Jesus Christ needs to be – and can be – related to the salvation of the whole creation and not only to that of human individuals. In our deliberations, we are now starting to consider not only the implications of being created and the relationship of the creation with its Creator, but also to think seriously about the functioning of the Creator Himself. In doing this we can start to answer the question of how a traditional Christian doctrine of God can address the questions posed by suffering and environmental damage.

4.1 Salvation as Creation

Christianity is a religion founded on the salvation wrought by Jesus Christ on the cross at the first Easter and His resurrection from the dead. Because of this it is often easy to overlook the fact that Christianity is concerned with creation as well as with salvation and that the two ideas are actually different aspects of the same basic insight into God. Creation and salvation are very closely related and have more in common with each other than has traditionally been taught within Christian theology.

The roots of the idea that God is continually creative and that creation and salvation are two aspects of a single process are to be found in the Old Testament. The fact that the concept of Heilsgeschichte or Salvation-History lead to the production of the creation narratives points in this direction, as does the nature of the divine name 'YHWH' as revealed to Moses in Exodus Ch.3.[1] God is what He will be and He acts in History for His own purposes. This was the insight into God which was grasped and proclaimed by the author of Isaiah Chapters 40-55; namely that God is the God who can act in a new way and create anew.[2]

Despite the Hebrew differentiation between *bara'* and *'asah*, that is, creation from nothing and creation from existing material, we can see the idea of God's continual creativity in the ongoing appearance of new forms within the cosmos. This is the view of the creation as an open system which contains future potentialities within itself.[3] The openness in creation which results in freedom and the potential for wrong and evil is the same openness which allows the continual action of the creator. Moltmann sees the idea of an initial creation linked to salvation-history, as pointing towards creation being a three stage process: creation in the beginning; creative acts within history; and the creation of the endtime.[4] This is a consequence of the idea that time, as well as space and matter, is a part of creation. Tillich expressed this idea as follows:

'Since the divine life is essentially creative, all three modes of time must be used in symbolizing it. God has created the world, he is creative in the present moment, and he will creatively fulfil his telos. Therefore we must speak of originating creation, sustaining creation, and directing creation'.[5]

Such a view is supported by a crucial verse from John's Gospel. In Ch.5 v17 Jesus states, 'My Father has been working up to the present'. In this statement the Greek grammatical construction carries the implication that this action will continue into the future. The New Testament scholar Charles Barrett has suggested that this verse reflects the thought of the Alexandrian Jewish philosopher and exegete Philo, who denied that God ever ceased His creative action, as well as rabbinic literature from the New Testament period.[6]

Tillich saw creation as being a part of God's nature; a nature in which creation and redemption belong together because redemption is a part of the creative process.[7] It could be argued that such claim seems to make creation necessary, whereas Christianity has traditionally opposed any necessity for God to act. However, Tillich disagreed with this argument, writing:

> 'God is creative because he is God. Therefore, it is meaningless to ask whether creation is a necessary or a contingent act of God. Nothing is necessary for God in the sense that he is dependent on a necessity above him. His aseity implies that everything which he is he is through himself. He eternally 'creates himself,' a paradoxical phrase which states God's freedom.[8]

The recognition that redemption is part of the creative process is important. It is not that creation occurred and that due to problems which then emerged that redemption became necessary, but rather that redemption was always part of the plan as an ongoing part of the process. Redemption is an integral part of the creative process which God took into account when He first began creation. It can be argued such discussions of God's nature so stretch our comprehension beyond its limits that it is better to say that God is creativity itself. The creative redemption which is found in God is the necessary corollary to the alienation which occurs in the human condition.[9] It is the answer to the alienation which we experience from that which is around about us and which is itself a manifestation of Original Sin (where Original Sin is defined in the manner described in chapter two). In our present context we should note that this alienation extends beyond humanity and includes the alienation between man and the world which is demonstrated by the environmental crisis which we have taken as our theological context.

This concept that creation and salvation are two aspects of the same activity was apparent to writers in the patristic period and found its classic expression in the words of Athanasius, who wrote:

'The renewal of the creation has been wrought by the self-same Word who made it in the beginning.'[10]

For Athanasius, the creative Word of God, as the agent of creation, was the only one who could bring about this renewal.[11] The action of God in the beginning and the action of God on the cross are two aspects of the same activity.

Just as creation is implicit in God, in the same way so are love and redemption. Moreover, although we can see creation as involving a decision on the part of God, any arbitrariness which this might seem to imply on His part can be removed by the premise that for God to have acted otherwise would have been to act against His own nature (see also section 3.3). It is possible for events to be inevitable without there being any compulsion placed upon their prime movers. Moltmann expresses this by noting that creation, as a self-communication of God's goodness, is part of His nature. There was no external agent compelling God to create; the creation was inevitable because of God's nature. If God was to restrict this nature, he would no longer be able to act freely but would instead be self-limited. God is therefore only acting freely when he acts according to His nature.[12]

In addressing the redemption of a creation which is under threat, this intrinsic divine creativity and the ways in which Moltmann and Tillich describe God's three stages of creation are important. Moltmann sees the initial creation as being effortless but the continued involvement in that creation as being far more demanding. He contrasts the effortless 'Let there be. . .' of the Priestly account in Genesis chapter one with the words of Isaiah Ch.43 v24 as God talks with His people. '. . . you have burdened me with your sins, you have wearied me with your iniquities.'[13] In His action in the world, God has to overcome the negative manifestations of the freedom which He has lovingly made a part of His creation and the way in which this negativity acts upon Him. If we see the Holy Spirit as indwelling all living things and as being the divine energy underlying the continuing process of creation, then in as much as the actions of humanity act against life on earth and restrict evolutionary potential, so they are also actions against the Holy Spirit and therefore actions against God Himself. Moreover, in overcoming these actions God has to act without in any way negating or restricting the freedom which he has lovingly bestowed on the whole of creation. The love of God means that He has had to take a risk in creation, for in allowing freedom He has made His own task more difficult and restricted the possible responses which he could make to that creaturely freedom.[14]

In his consideration of the love of God and of our response to that love, Bill Vanstone has noted three characteristics of true love and reflected on their implications for God's creativity if that creativity is rooted in His love.[15] The first of these is that true love is never limited; God imposes no interior limit on His own self-giving. God holds back nothing in His continual creative activity. He spends Himself to the utmost for that which He has made. He is wholly committed to His creation and devotes His whole self to it. The second characteristic is that since love is given freely, it never seeks to control that to which it is given. In creation, this results in the potential for both triumph and disaster – the freedom which we have discussed above. The triumph of human freedom can be seen in the conquest of disease, and the disaster which results from human freedom in the damage done to the natural environment. The third characteristic is that in its giving, true love is costly and can never be completely detached. There is always an involvement of the lover with the recipient of that love. This results in a creative activity which is vulnerable and which can be frustrated by the response of the very creation to which the love is given. God is not far off, but near. God's transcendence is balanced by His immanence. This can be described as the vulnerability of the creative love of God. (We should note that Vanstone draws back from describing God Himself as vulnerable, because it is God's activity which we experience rather than God's inner self.)[16]

These ideas about creative love are closely related to those involved with the concept of 'play'. It could be argued that because we use the word 'play' to describe contrived games and activities, we stand in danger of losing the idea of what play is really about and the nature of its genuine characteristics. In the present context, play could be described as free and spontaneous activity which is completely absorbing of those who are involved and which, whilst not being necessary, is directed towards a purpose. This description not only fits the play of small children, but is also very close to the way in which we have been describing creation: namely a free and spontaneous action on the part of God, which is both open to the future and also contains new possibilities. It also describes the insight into the love of God which Vanstone gained from his observation of two boys constructing a scenic model.[17]

Play also contains the commitment of those involved to the activity in question; a commitment which we could describe as love. Indeed, Moltmann has examined the ways in which play has been seen as a symbol of the redemption of the World.[18] Play can be a means of coming to terms with the unknown and the uncertainty of the future before this uncertainty has to be faced in reality. This is the truth which often lies behind children's so-called 'games of make-believe', which are really far from being make-believe at all.

The love which is implicit in commitment finds its expression in the faithfulness of God. A faithfulness which God expressed in the covenant which He made with His people and which was explored by St. Paul as he examined the relationship between the human and the divine. This concept of the faithfulness of God to that which He has created, is closely linked to the concept of the righteousness of God (δικαιοσυνη θεου – dikaiosune Theou). This righteousness is cognate with the Hebrew understanding expressed in words derived from the root *sdq* and was a concept used to express the fact that God does justice to the relationships in which He stands. In the present context it expresses the idea that having entered into a relationship through His creative activity, God will continue to be involved in intimate detail and will not stand idly by whilst the product of His creative action suffers. God will continue to be active in and through His creation irrespective of the threats which it may face and when these occur.

4.2 Salvation and Suffering

The threat to God's creation, which we have described as the vulnerability of the creative love of God, is seen by the Taiwanese theologian Choan-Seng Song as causing God pain. He writes: 'God's heart aches. His heart aches because of an immediate danger to creation'.[19] For Song, creation and redemption are two sides of the same coin, with creation as God's redemptive response to the pain and suffering in the world, and redemption as God's continuous response to creation. 'God's heart aches when the world is gripped with pain and suffering'; and for Song, this heartache is the beginning of theology.[20] The fact that God suffers is shown to us by the suffering of Christ on the cross, and we can see this suffering as the beginning of our redemption and of our thereby becoming a new creation.[21] Song sees this suffering as being implicit in the description of God as αγαπη (agape), an overwhelming benevolent love (1 John Ch.4 v16). This is the same love which Vanstone describes and which we linked to play and commitment in section 4.1.

The hope which Song finds in this theology is provided by the resurrection. Without God's suffering actually leading somewhere, there would be little hope either for humanity or for the creation as a whole. Song sees God searching out the lost elements in His creation in the same way as He called His people home in the Old Testament via His *hesedh* (steadfast love).[22] He describes this activity as 'pain-love' (a translation of the Chinese *thun-ai*), drawing insights from the Japanese theologian Kazoh Kitamori, who saw the heart of the gospel as being revealed through the pain of God.[23] Song, however, takes issue with Kitamori's argument that the love of God is rooted in His pain. He prefers to see the pain of God as being rooted in His love.[24] God's appreciation of the content of pain arises from His fundamental love rather than His love being a consequence of His experience of pain.

Dietrich Bonhoeffer and Jurgan Moltmann have both expressed similar ideas to those of Song. Shortly before his execution by the Nazis in 1945 Bonhoeffer wrote that God 'is weak and powerless in the world, and that is precisely the way, the only way, in which he is with us and helps us.'[25] Moltmann's trinitarian theology carries the claim that 'The cross on Golgotha has revealed the eternal heart of the Trinity'.[26] The problem is that we need to ask whether the present argument and the arguments of Moltmann are producing a modalistic patrology in which the suffering and characteristics of the Son are all ascribed to the Father, with the implication that the Son is simply a representation of the Father. This is a criticism which Nicholls has levelled at Moltmann.[27] Although our ruling premise that the Trinity is essential to our present theology, safeguards us from the modalism which was put forward by patristic writers such as Noetus and Sabellius, what of the question of a suffering Father?

If the idea of God the Father safeguards the transcendence of God in the Doctrine of The Trinity, then we could argue that in this respect God does not suffer. However, it is clear that Christ suffered on the cross, and our arguments have suggested that God as Holy Spirit encounters suffering in the creation. If the union of the three persons in the Trinity is described by love, then it would seem that the Father encounters suffering within this trinitarian relationship. Although the nature of this relationship is beyond our understanding, it might be helpful to consider that the Father, representing the transcendent aspect of the Trinity, does not suffer directly but knows suffering through His relationship of equals with the Son and the Holy Spirit.[28] The way in which the doctrine of the Trinity can be related to the theme of the suffering of God will be considered in more detail in section 5.2. We should also note that these ideas of divine suffering are far from alien to the teaching of the New Testament. The suffering of Jesus is only made possible by the self-giving love of God, as is observed in verse 14 of chapter three of John's gospel. It is this love which leads to the possibility of the pain of Christ on the cross.

Marcel Sarot has examined the ways in which the doctrine of the impassibility of God has come to be challenged and has examined it beginning with the premise that the God whom we meet in Christ is a suffering God.[29] Sarot notes that there are two arguments to support this premise of a suffering God, both drawing on the suffering of Jesus Christ on the cross. The first argument is that Christ is God incarnate so that Christ's suffering in the Incarnation implies that God Himself can suffer too. The second argument is that Christ reveals God to us so that Christ's suffering is a revelation of the suffering of God. Sarot's conclusion is that the second argument is valid, but that the first is flawed since it rests on an imperfect understanding of christology.

Sarot argues that although attributes are shared between the human and the divine natures in Christ (the concept of the *communicatio idiomatum*) and that although passibility or the ability to suffer is one of these attributes, this sharing applies only to the concrete person, to the final persona (what the Council of Chalcedon called the προσωπον, prosopon), and not to the abstract, to the individual natures. The Logos, the Word of God, truly suffered in its concrete Incarnation, but this does not necessarily imply that the divine nature suffered in itself and it cannot therefore be concluded by this argument that the Father and the Holy Spirit also suffer.

Sarot's argument rests on the precise definition of the *communicatio idiomatum* and this has a very fine dividing line. The Oxford Dictionary of the Christian Church appears to contradict Sarot in its discussion, but omits to give the definition of the Chalcedonian Settlement which described Christ as existing 'in two natures' (εν δυο φυσεσι), with the exchange of attributes occurring in the προσωπον.[30] By the definition of Cyril of Alexandria who ascribed all of Christ's experience to the single subject of the divine Word of God, Sarot would be wrong, but by the definition of The Council of Chalcedon he would be correct. Perhaps Sarot should have used the original language and terminology rather than terms such as concrete and abstract, for as Aquinas noted, God is actually neither.

Having dismissed the first argument in support of the suffering of God, based on the Incarnation, Sarot accepts the second, namely that we know that God suffers because Jesus is the perfect revelation of God. As a result, if Jesus suffered, so too did God, irrespective of whether Jesus was himself divine. If Sarot is correct and this argument based on revelation is valid, then it has an interesting consequence. This is, that if we are to answer Anselm's question, 'Cur Deus Homo?' (Why did God become man?) then it is no good claiming that God became man in order to show that He suffers with the world and to show the love of God – claims which are often made within liberal theology. It may well be true that the incarnate Word does do this, but within this liberal argument the Incarnation was not necessary in order to show this suffering of God, since the revelation does not rely on Jesus being divine. Nor was the incarnation necessary in order for God to know suffering, since it is claimed that He knew this already. It seems that if God knows suffering and we accept the doctrine of the Incarnation, then we are driven to an objective view of the atonement in which the death of Christ on the cross actually achieves something. This in turn implies that there was something to achieve and leads us back to the deeper truths of sin and evil which, as we have already noted, are too often dismissed within the liberal theological tradition.

However, expressions of the idea that God can suffer, such as those outlined above, have been criticised as being grotesque by writers such as Don Cupitt.[31] Cupitt attacks what he sees as the God of Modern Patripassionism, making partic- ular reference to the works of Studdert-Kennedy. He sees this as the God of humanism, a figure made in our own image who reflects the suffering which we experience in the world. He goes so far as to describe this as an inadequate god, 'not a god at all'. Although he has himself dispensed with what he terms a 'Realist God', Cupitt also notes that 'at least the Realist God was religiously adequate.'

Such arguments contain several flaws. First, they do not do justice to the concept of what the suffering of God actually means, both in terms of the fact that the Christian God is not unitarian but triune and also because they fail to address the question of what we mean when we apply human adjectives to the Divine (see chapter six). Secondly, arguments such as those of Cupitt are flawed because he posits that this God is inadequate because He reflects our own suffering, and yet Cupitt has already dismissed a realist understanding of God, preferring instead to understand God as a projection of the human mind. He claims that the mind produces this projection in order to satisfy its own psychological needs. According to

Cupitt, God is not real, being instead the result of a projection of our own needs, but God could not suffer, because that would be a projection of our own suffering.

It can also be argued that suffering is the flaw in the discussion concerning God's eternal creativity. The question which needs to be answered here is this: In Jesus' cry of dereliction from the cross, when His words implied that God appeared to have forsaken him, was Jesus truly separated from the love of God and if so did the divine creativity cease at this point in time and space? Moreover, if creativity did cease in space and time, what does this imply about the creativity of God in eternity, given that the cross is the manifestation in space and time of what is an eternal truth?

As with the overall question of the atonement, there is no complete and satisfactory answer to these questions. Yet analysis of the questions shows that they miss two vital points. The first is that the figure on the cross was not merely human, but also divine. God takes the alienation of the universe to Himself, and does not simply cut off His relationship with a human figure as the question supposes. The second is that we have identified creation and salvation as a single activity; they are two different facets of one operation. If this is the case, then the question resolves itself, for the cry of dereliction of Christ on the cross is right at the heart of the salvific action of God. God's creative activity may appear to be absent, but His salvific action is never more apparent. The result is that there is no discontinuity in the ongoing activity of creation-salvation. It can also be argued that the opposition which is often voiced to the idea that God can suffer or feel pain is based on a low doctrine of the Trinity. It results from a lack of understanding of the importance of this doctrine and of the insights which it provides into God.

Returning to the question of salvation and redemption (and thence to the cross and the resurrection) we should note that because this is now seen as an integral part of God's creative activity, then it is actually an essential activity, rather than a divine rescue operation for a fallen creation. Put another way, the cross was always going to be there: it was an integral part of what was involved in the creative activity and not some last-ditch solution to an unexpected emergency. Although it is also

far more than this, the cross does act as an expressive demonstration of just how great the love of God is, as Vanstone has
observed in his 'A Hymn to the Creator'.[32] The cross is an
integral part of God's methodology, given the freedom which
He has given to that creation.[33] We can take this idea further
and note Grace Jantzen's idea that suffering cannot be justified
by subsequent reward alone:

> 'All the joys of heaven cannot justify previous pain and
> suffering unless those joys are in some way a direct result
> of the suffering, not just as compensating rewards, but as
> intrinsically impossible without the pain.'[34]

Jantzen is arguing that pain and suffering can only be justified
if they are an essential part of the coming into being of the
Kingdom of God. This statement is arrogant in that it refuses
to let God have purposes beyond our understanding, an admission which Job was finally compelled to make. Yet it is also
possible that we are moving towards an explication of Jantzen's
claim, when we note that freedom and creation-salvation are
both manifestations of the same feature of the universe; a
feature which scientists have described through the second law
of thermodynamics. God's action on the cross is an affirmation
of this freedom and creativity as God takes the consequences
of this freedom to Himself.[35]

4.3 Salvation and Jesus Christ

Holding onto the doctrine of the Trinity, we must now note the
part of Jesus Christ in the trinitarian vision of salvation and
creation. Alistair McFadyen has written that an abstract theory
of the Trinity as a model to follow and to rule our lives, does
little to liberate, speaks of no grace and cannot empower us,
irrespective of the form which this doctrine takes.[36] This is the
case because of our fallen human nature. At this point we can
again echo Anselm, and ask that if the doctrine of The Trinity
could inspire us in this way, then why would the incarnation
have been necessary at all; 'Cur Deus Homo?' Perhaps it is
because of the abstract way in which the Trinity has often been

presented that it seems irrelevant to so many people. The relevance and activity of the Trinity needs to be made more apparent if this is indeed the God in whom we claim to believe.

In chapter three, we noted the ideas of Ross Thompson concerning the Father and Holy Spirit and the way in which they can express transcendence and immanence. Within this structure Thompson sees Incarnation as 'a step away from an incomprehensible immanence into an otherness we can grasp.' He continues,

> 'The transcendent God is nowhere in particular, because as immanent he is everywhere; to grasp him, we need him incarnate somewhere. As transcendent he is eternal, because as immanent, every moment is charged with his presence; to know him we need him at some particular time in our history.'[37]

Ross Thompson makes the point that an immanent God who is only present in all places and at all times (as the gods of panentheism and Process Theology would be) is just as intangible as a wholly transcendent God who is not present at all. It is in the unique physicality of the Incarnation at a specific place and at a specific time that God is able to be known. A different way of expressing the same idea is to realise that God the transcendent Father does not have a point of view, only points to view,[38] and yet if we are to communicate with the divine or to grasp anything of His true meaning then we must encounter Him in a particular point of view, a need met in the Incarnation.

This argument is related to Wolfhart Pannenberg's claim that for the Incarnation, the fact and its interpretation are one,[39] so that the meaning of the Incarnation is present within the event itself; the event which is the entry of the divine into history at one particular place and time. For Pannenberg, we can narrow the crucial event down further and locate it in the resurrection, which can be seen as both speaking of the eschatological expectations of time, and as being a prolepsis (a present foretaste of a future event) of that which is to come. History is moving forwards into eschatology and the Christian faith and eschatological expectations are irrevocably connected.

Tom Torrance has followed a similar line of argument to that of Pannenberg. He notes that whatever the actions of God are, they must have empirical correlates within history if God is to be in any way understood within space-time. Torrance relates how Barth, who had earlier seen the resurrection as Geschichte and therefore as a real but an ahistorical event, was later to note 'Mark well, bodily resurrection', implying that the resurrection also has an element in the historie of space-time, that is, that it can be known within human history.[40] The resurrection is both an event within history and an event which is beyond space and time as we know them. We would do well to note the words of St. Paul from the 15th chapter of his first letter to Corinth. 'If Christ has not been raised, then our preaching is in vain and your faith is in vain. We are even found to be misrepresenting God.' However, the Biblical vision goes further than Incarnation alone, through the development of eschatological doctrine and the vision of the Cosmic Christ.[41]

Moltmann has noted how the Church can so easily lose sight of the links between christology and eschatology, writing that the division of the two has been present from the earliest days of the Church.[42] As time went by, Jesus came to be seen as a divine figure who came into the world to save sinners, with the on-going work of the Spirit and the return of Christ being neglected. Salvation became a personalised process and the last-judgement was replaced by individual death. Such an approach both misses out on the continual creation-salvation of God in history, and also leaves little hope for a creation which is damaged through malpractice.

Christian teaching which has focused on human salvation and ignored the rest of creation may well be the one area in which Christian Theology is truly guilty of a misplaced anthropocentrism. Salvation in Jesus Christ can speak of a movement of all creation beyond the historical process. As Moltmann has noted, we need to turn from anthropocentrism to christocentrism; we need to turn from ecclesiocentricity to theocentricity.[43] The historical experiences of Christ can only be of all-embracing significance if we see them against the background of the creation-salvation of the Universe and can relate them to the salvation of the whole of that universe. This is the concept of the 'Cosmic Christ', that the second person of the Trinity is before all, after all and for all. As Hans Urs von Balthasar put it, 'the concrete expression of God in the created cosmos and the *raptus* which carries this entire cosmos back to God, are both fulfilled in the Person of the Son.'[44]

In Colossians Ch.1 vv15-20, we find that not only were all things created in Christ, but that all things are reconciled to God through Christ. The writer of the letter to the Ephesians took this slightly further when he wrote that God's plan for the fullness of time is to unite all things in Christ (Ephesians Ch.1 v10). It is not certain who wrote these letters to Colossae and Ephesus, but in I Corinthians Ch.8 v6 we also find St. Paul writing that all things are from God the Father for whom we exist and that all things come through Jesus Christ through whom we exist. These references indicate that the reconciliation applies to all things, not only to humanity, and can therefore be seen as the liberation of creation. We are here referring to the extension of the concept of κοινονια (communion) beyond its perfect presence in the Holy Trinity (and its imperfect presence in human relationships and the human relationship with God), so that it characterises perfectly all relationships within the creation. The grace of God extends to all that He has made and not simply to the human race. This is an idea which was largely neglected by the Western Church (other than in the Celtic Tradition), but which is now being rediscovered as we see its relevance to a World under threat.

Polkinghorne notes that this is the essence which lies behind the move from a world in which pain and death occur to one in which they are absent. This is concomitant with a move from a universe in which God allows creation the freedom to stand against Him (and thereby have the potential for evil and decay) to a universe in which independence is relinquished in favour of a more intimate relationship with the Father.[45] This is a state which can be attained only through a return of the present creation, rather than starting from scratch – *ex vetero* rather than *ex nihilo*. The resurrection was the first taste of this. Any argument that this re-creation removes freedom can be countered by the argument that it will only be granted to those who desire it – a variation on the traditional idea that heaven is only entered by those people who deserve to enter it. Augustine of Hippo would have argued that the removal of the potential to do wrong is not a restriction of freedom if the person concerned has no desire to do wrong.

Arguments such as that above allow us to come to terms with the troublesome verse seven in chapter 45 of The Book of Isaiah, in which God states that He creates darkness and woe. These are the natural consequences of a universe in which freedom exists and in which there is no restriction on the place of operation of the Holy Spirit. Although Origen disagreed with the notion that the Holy Spirit could operate in inanimate objects, with the breath of Genesis Ch.2 v7 being reserved for the saints (i.e. the Church), this view was later opposed by Athanasius and the Cappadocian Fathers.[46]

In this context it is important to note that Christ is the saviour of the World (or rather the Universe) and not of the Church. This is the fundamental fact of the idea of the Cosmic Christ. Anyone who believes that Christ is against other groups and sees Him exclusively as the possession of their own group has not grasped the Christian Gospel.[47] In New Testament theology, Christ is contrasted with Adam, the father of the human race, rather than with Abraham, the father of Judaism. This also ties in with Teilhard de Chardin's description of Christ as the 'Omega Point', a product of the cosmic evolutionary process through his humanity, yet also outside this process through His divinity.[48] In this, Christ embraced the whole of creation. Teilhard de Chardin wrote: 'Christ must be kept as large as creation and remain its head. No matter how large we discover the world to be, the figure of Jesus, risen from the dead, must embrace it in its entirety'.[49] This has to be the final rejection of anthropocentrism and the recognition that the whole creation finds a place in the work of Christ, just as all came into being from the creative Word of God. It is not that Christianity has to be integrated to the World, but rather that Christ embraces the whole World and takes it to Himself.

4.4 Salvation in Time and beyond Time

Because salvation and creation are both aspects of the same activity of God, then salvation can be understood in two different ways. There is the salvation which is wrought within time and space through the continual divine creative action, and there is the salvation which is beyond space and time. We therefore need to ask how salvation can grow out of the present situation as well as how it can be imposed from the outside.

The first of these questions is answered through the idea of the perfection of The Kingdom of God. In Luke Ch.4 vv18-20, Jesus claimed to be the fulfilment of the prophecy from Isaiah Ch.61. Writers such as Bishop Hugh Montefiore have noted that the Church has too often emphasised the New Testament teaching on eschatological judgement at the expense of the teaching on the Kingdom of God (or Heaven) which we find in the Gospels. The claim is made that it is this Kingdom which holds out the promise of redemption, or liberation, for the whole of creation.[50] The Kingdom of God is thereby seen as the fulfilment of creation within the present world system, the fulfilment of a creation which is open to the future, despite the continual closing of God's open system by the actions of humanity (see the discussion by Moltmann).[51] In theological terms, the Kingdom of God is here seen as being realised in the future of the present world.

The second way of viewing salvation is in terms of the consummation of eschatological hope. This again results from the opening of closed systems, but this time the opening is performed by God in a way which transforms the creation.[52] This Kingdom again exists in the future, but this time it is separated in some way from the present World. Taken together, these two futures represent the redemption of the whole creation anticipated by St. Paul in chapter eight of his letter to the Romans (verses 18-23).

Here Paul writes of the salvation of the whole of creation (κτισισ) and not simply of humanity. He also notes that the creation was not subjected to pain willingly (ουκ εκουσα), but through the subjecting one (δια τον῾υποταξαντα), a reference which Dunn links with his understanding of the fall of man through Adam.[53] There is a human responsibility for the plight of the creation which is implicit in the whole of the created order. Creation is to be freed from this slavery to decay, in order that it may enter into the freedom of the children of God.

In this vision, God is extending the promise of His covenant not only from Jew to Gentile, but also to the whole of the created order so as to redeem the whole universe. The fate of the whole of the 'good' creation is at stake and what the writer of Ecclesiastes saw as a vain cycle of life and death is here transformed through the action of the Word of God. It is in Jesus Christ the man that we see how the created order can relate to the Father in Sonship and thereby gain eternal life. It is through Jesus Christ, both existentially and ontologically (i.e. both through experience and in itself) that creation is brought into and knows sonship with its creator.

Taking up these ideas, Gustavo Gutierrez noted that humanity is called to work with God in a continuation of the work wrought by Christ – a work which is both creative and salvific.[54] This is the positive action which results from a modern theology of creation and is none other than the liberation of the creation from the bondage in which it has been placed by man through the misuse of our freedom. This can be understood as placing an obligation upon the human race to act in such a way as to remove that bondage. Such an obligation removes the possibility that an escapist appeal to eschatological action will solve all our problems for us. The human race should not ignore ecological damage on the grounds that God will sort it all out eventually, just as it cannot justify killing people on the grounds that this does not matter because they will receive compensation beyond death in The Kingdom of God.

We are called upon to work for the realisation of the Kingdom of God on earth, whilst realising that we can never achieve it by our own efforts. This failure is a consequence of our fallen nature and also a consequence of the second law of thermodynamics. We are inevitably estranged from our full potential for good. Perfection is not humanly achievable, and this applies as much to the eradication of pollution as it does to the nature of human relationships and a perfect communion with God. Ultimately, we do have to look to the hope of an eschatological future and to the expectation that space and time as we know it will cease. Unlike Process Theology, which sees solutions as evolving in the present from the past, a full doctrine of the Trinity allows us to look to the future and to a time when God will act in what could be called a new way.

This expression 'New Way' is actually a misnomer, for whatever the divine action, it will still be a part of God's ongoing creation-salvation. Indeed, since the eschatological activity which we are now considering is actually activity outside time, it is not necessary to restrict its application to a point at the end of time. From our perspective such events (if we can describe them as such) will be at the end of time, but from a perspective where time is not a constraint this need not be the case and can be understood as part of God's ongoing creative purpose. This is a further expression of what we noted in section 2.4, namely that the Creation and the Covenant are inseparable, as are Redemption and the Cross. Such 'New Creation' finds its full expression in the Christian doctrine of the resurrection; the promise made by God in Christ. The resurrection can be seen as the opening up of the promise and possibility of the redemption of space-time.

When we apply the ideas of the resurrection to human individuals we again need to clarify our understanding. The doctrine of the resurrection means more than the mere continued existence of some sort of ethereal soul. It also involves the resurrection of the body. Resurrection is to a substantial 'existence' in whatever sort of physicality is appropriate to the New Creation. Too much emphasis has been given to the concept of a 'soul' by earlier generations and this has led to what some commentators have described as a mind-body dualism on the part of Christianity. If we want to retain the language of the soul because we find it helpful or because it has become a part of our heritage and our habitual religious language, then it needs a redefinition. Indeed, if the concept can be understood in the light of a more balanced theology it can have an important part to play both in understanding personal recognisability and in answering the question of what happens in the time between the grave and the resurrection.

If the resurrected body is recognisable as whoever it was in this present existence, then there must be some recollection or memory after death, so that in some sense the 'essence' of that person continues. Helen Oppenheimer has suggested that this recollection could be referred to as the soul.[55] In this context we would do well to adopt Oppenheimer's view that in the resurrection, 'God consecrates a new body to me'. This understanding means that it becomes possible to talk both about the resurrection of the dead at the end of History, and also about the resurrection of a dead person as if it had already happened. Because they have left time, the eternal potential is open to them. A spatial analogy makes this clear: If I journey to a foreign country, then the country exists before I get there.

If we extend these ideas and apply them to the whole of creation rather than simply to human individuals, then the implications become too great for us to imagine. We are faced with the prospect that as this world decays, some elements within it remain with the Divine, so that the 'New Creation' shares recognisable similarities with the old. Perhaps this recognisability comes from the fact that they are both the products of the same creator.

The other manifestation of the endtime which we should note is that of the return of Christ (his second coming). Tillich noted that this idea above all others was the Christian claim to answer the World problem in a way that other religions could not, for Christ at the end of History transcends all History.[56] If the return of Christ marks the end of History, then there is no superior manifestation of the divine. This argument applies just as much to the Christian perspective on the supremacy of Christ over New-Age religious movements. Christ transcends anything which the world can offer. In the ecological context, the only full solution must have the same origins as the creation. This is the solution which occurs at the end of time in the new creation.

The idea of Christ returning at the end of History does not merely point to Him transcending History. It is a mark of the fact that the transcendence of God can act in creation in a way which would not be possible if He was only present within that creation. Eschatology and resurrection are only compatible with a God who is in some way transcendent, for they require a God who is in some way separate from that which exists in a created sense. Process Theology and pantheism cannot offer such a hope, for in identifying God with the 'creation', they have bound His fate with that of the universe. There is no external agent to act from outside the closed system.

There is no need for us to see the eschaton as a sudden event which transforms the universe in an instant. Whilst it can be argued that those theologians such as Bultmann who posit that eschatology has to do with the present time and this world, fail to recognise the nature of the world and the presence of Original Sin, this does not mean that God is idle and not working his purposes out in the present day. If creation is not only a past event, but also extends through the present into the future, then it can also be true that the consummation of history extends from the future back into the present of our own day. There is a continuity between the present space-time in which we live and the new creation; a continuity which is evident in the way in which space and time are transformed. In each case it allows us to incorporate the insights of salvation history.

This approach, which owes much to Pannenberg and Moltmann, should be distinguished from the ideas of process theology. Now, God is beyond the creation as well as being active within it; He is true to His eternal self, rather than being wholly a part of the process of change. Nor does this approach rule out a major change in the created order. It simply recognises what we have been stressing throughout this chapter, namely that salvation is an action of the divine within history as God acts to annul the effects of the negative possibilities which are a part of the creation. However, these arguments should not preclude us from asking whether we can find the first-fruits of this salvation in our present situation, and if so, how we are to find them. For if we can find these first-fruits, then they can be utilised as a part of our working with God towards a present realisation of The Kingdom.

For St. Paul, such evidence was to be found in the giving of the Holy Spirit (e.g. Romans Ch.8 v23). The resurrection of Jesus Christ can be seen as a stage in God's saving action for His people. Moltmann finds the first-fruits in the Sabbath, which he sees as the feast-day of creation.[57] He notes that in the Priestly creation narrative, the writer saw seven days of creation (both *bara'* and *'asah*), the seventh being the day when God rested. As such, God can be seen as creating rest on the Sabbath day as the completion of His creation.[58] This idea of rest is one which is increasingly lost on humanity, being seen in the context of the decalogue (the ten commandments), where it is given as a commandment, rather than in the context of the creation narrative in Genesis Ch.1-2, where it can be seen as an aspect of human activity which is in the image of God. It is also increasingly being lost as the days of the week become more uniform and as special days of rest, prayer or recreation are lost, irrespective of the religious or social tradition from which they originate.

There is more to the idea of the Sabbath than that of human rest. The decalogue in Exodus chapter 20 makes it clear that its provisions also apply to cattle used as beasts of labour. This idea was extended to the whole of creation through the concept of the Sabbath year and the year of Jubilee when the land was left uncultivated and thereby allowed to rest.[59] The Sabbath can be seen as a time when man rests from his exploitation of the creation and allows it too to rest. This ideal holds both the prospect of a present reality and the foretaste of what may be to come. It is present in the vision of the writer of Isaiah Ch.61 where he sees the year of the Lord's favour, an eschatological expression of the idea of the Year of Jubilee.[60] We would also do well to remind ourselves that eschatology applies to time as well as to space.

Despite these arguments, we must not lose sight of the present problem. The human race is causing potentially irreversible damage to creation. A Christian approach to this problem needs to maintain what Gabriel Daly calls a High Christology and a High Eschatology, which do not reduce the scope of the redemptive power of Christ nor the action of God.[61] Yet in doing this we need to do justice to the conviction that not only does salvation demand divine action, but also that God is active and present in all that happens in His creation. Creation allows evil to challenge God and we must expect that God does and will reply; not only in transcendent power, but also in an immanent sharing of the suffering of His creation. The cross is the sign that He does not just watch as an idle spectator, but that He is active and involved in the suffering. We must also not lose sight of the fact that the Church (in its widest sense) is a pilgrim people, continually searching and journeying; open to creative change. Such a church not only has to embrace the suffering which we are inflicting on the world and play its part in determining the action which will lead to the liberation of the creation, but it must also ensure that its own internal assumptions, its theology and its language are not and do not become part of the problem. We have already noted the low priority given to the doctrine of The Trinity in much Christian teaching and we must now explore this doctrine and its implications in more detail.

Notes

1. For a discussion of the name YHWH, see the discussion in Chapter 3.3 as well as Von Rad (1975) pp.136ff and pp.179ff.
2. E.g. Isaiah Ch.43.v18.
3. E.g. Peacocke (1979) pp.79f.
4. Moltmann (1979) pp.118f; (1981) p.209; (1985) pp.206ff.
5. Tillich (1978a) p.253. The word 'telos' expresses the idea of inner-meaning.
6. Barrett pp.255f.
7. Tillich (1978a) p.252ff.
8. Tillich (1978a) p.252.
9. E.g. Daly (1988) pp.195f.
10. Athanasius 'De Incarnatione Verbi Dei', Ch.1.
11. Athanasius op. cit. Ch.7.
12. Moltmann (1985) pp.80ff.
13. Moltmann (1985) p.210.
14. See also Peacocke (1979) pp.198ff.
15. Vanstone (1977) pp.39ff and pp.57ff.
16. Vanstone (1977) p.66.
17. Vanstone (1977) pp.30ff.
18. Moltmann (1985) pp.310ff.
19. Song p.35.
20. Song p.40.
21. Song pp.48ff echoing II Corinthians Ch.5 v17.
22. Song pp.64ff who cites Jer. Ch.3 vv12–13 and Hosea Ch.11 v8.
23. Song pp.59ff quoting Kitamori pp.19f.
24. Song p.67.
25. Bonhoeffer (1971) pp.360f.
26. Moltmann (1981) pp.25 and 31ff.
27. Nicholls pp.238–239; see also Moltmann (1974) p.265.
28. This issue has been discussed in a number of places, e.g. Moltmann (1974) pp.235ff, and (1981) pp.21ff.
29. See the article by Sarot.
30. See Kelly pp.338ff or Stevenson pp.350ff.
31. See e.g. Cupitt (1980).

32. Vanstone (1977) pp.119f. See also Oppenheimer (1983) p.5.
33. Daly (1988) pp.24f.
34. Jantzen (1987) pp.186ff.
35. See also Carr pp.122ff.
36. McFadyen (1992) pp.13–14.
37. R. Thompson (1992) p.24.
38. An observation which is made by Fynn.
39. Pannenburg, 'The Revelation of God in Jesus of Nazareth', writing in Robinson and Cobb, pp.126–7. Quoted on pp.18–19 of Macquarrie (1990).
40. See T.Torrance (1976). In simple terms, the word 'Geschichte' is used to refer to events which are ahistorical, in which God impinges on the world from eternity, and the word 'historie' is used to refer to events which occur within history as we see it.
41. For a recent account of this subject see Moltmann (1990), pp.274–312.
42. Moltmann (1990) pp.3–5.
43. Moltmann (1990) p.276.
44. Von Balthaser (1986) p.56.
45. Polkinghorne (1991) pp.102f.
46. The views of Origen can be found in De Principiis, *1*,3.6–7.
47. Moltmann (1990) p.276.
48. Teilhard de Chardin pp.270ff; Daly (1988) p.77.
49. For this quotation from Teilhard de Chardin, see Daly (1988) p.94.
50. Montefiore pp.61ff.
51. Moltmann (1985) p.63; (1981) p.209.
52. Moltmann (1985) pp.118ff.
53. See Dunn pp.470ff.
54. Guterriez pp.158ff.
55. These ideas are usefully discussed by Helen Oppenheimer in her article 'Ourselves and Our Bodies', Oppenheimer (1991).
56. Tillich (1978b) p.163.
57. Moltmann (1985) pp.6, 276ff and discussed throughout Ch.XI
58. Moltmann (1985) p.276.
59. Leviticus Ch.25. See also Moltmann (1985) p.285 and 289.
60. See also Moltmann (1985) p.289.
61. Daly (1988) pp.210ff.

Chapter 5

God The Holy Trinity

In the preceding chapters, we have examined the nature of the environmental crisis which the world is now facing, the ways in which God's transcendence and immanence are important when considering His relationship with His creation and the divine response to this situation. This response has been described in terms of salvation and suffering. In doing this, we have drawn very much on traditional Christian doctrine and we have attempted to show that such doctrine is able to address the present problems in ways which are relevant and which mean that we do not need to develop new doctrines to cope with these environmental issues.

In particular, the doctrine of The Trinity has been used in several places in an attempt to show that traditional Christian teaching can address the present environmental crisis. However, it has also been contended that there is a widespread lack of understanding both of The Trinity itself and also of its relevance and importance in answering the questions which are being asked at the present time. If this contention is correct, then what can we say about the Trinity which is neither simplistic nor excessively complex and which is also consistent with the recent resurgence in mainstream theological thinking on this subject?[1] In answering this question we firstly consider the way in which the doctrine has developed and then examine how the doctrine can be a part of the Christian response to the current environmental crisis.

5.1 The Trinity in History

If we are to speak about God in a way which is true to traditional Christian doctrine, then we need to do so in terms of the Trinity. John Thompson has noted that we should not be able to speak of God apart from the Trinity for that is who God is;[2] a view which echoes the opinion of the Cappadocian Fathers, that for the Christian the word God means Father, Son and Holy Spirit.[3] If we accept this argument, then we need to examine the ways in which we understand the Doctrine of the Trinity so that we can apply it in our present context.[4] According to Gregory Nazianzus, there are two Christian doctrines, the validity of which should not be open to question. One of these is the Doctrine of the Trinity, the other The Incarnation.[5]

Yet despite the centrality of these doctrines, the language we use for both the Incarnation and the Trinity can often be misleading. The statement that God became man may well be correct, but it is also imprecise and expresses little of the actual content of the Christian doctrine as well as being misleading on the subject of the Trinity. It is a statement which could just as easily made by a unitarian believer (a person who does not acknowledge the divinity of the Word of God and of the Holy Spirit). It may also be an example of the way in which the language which we use feeds popular belief and results in a distortion of doctrine.

It took several centuries for the early Church to formulate the doctrine of God the Holy Trinity in a coherent manner. Its earliest recorded usage is as a formula (Father, Son and Holy Ghost) used both at baptism and in the Eucharist. Chapter 28 of Matthew's Gospel contains a baptismal formula in its nineteenth verse and in the middle of the second century Justin Martyr quoted both a baptismal formula and words from the Eucharist in his 'Apologies for the Christian Faith', (chapters 61 and 65 respectively).[6] In this usage it would appear that the Doctrine of The Trinity grew out of doxological practice rather than theological discussion, a view which has been discussed by Moltmann.[7] The main theological interests at the time were an apology for Christianity in a pagan world, together with a growing discussion on Christology.

It was not until Tertullian's treatise 'Against Praxeas', circa AD 213, that the term 'trinitas' itself was used, along with Tertullian's formula 'una substantia – tres personae' (one substance – three persons). It is notable for our purposes that Tertullian derived this expression from a consideration of God's economy of creation and salvation in the world; what we would now call Salvation History. If Tertullian could use God's economy of creation and salvation as the basis for his trinitarian theology, we should be able to use that same Trinity to address issues of salvation and creation in the present day. The Cappadocian Fathers, who were arguably the greatest trinitarian theologians of their time, also used Salvation History to support their development of the Trinity, a fact which is again discussed by Moltmann.[8]

The Doctrine of The Trinity was formally accepted at the Council of Constantinople in AD 381 when the consubstantiality (or 'ομοουσιον – homo-ousion) of the Holy Spirit was endorsed. The Trinity had survived some three hundred years of theological controversy and discussion to emerge as a formal part of Christian doctrine and belief. Although this late date could be seen as implying that the doctrine was a late development, it had been in everyday doxological use since the first century and seems to have been an implicit part of Christian belief even if it was not formally codified. As the Scottish theologian John Thompson puts it, echoing Barth's Church Dogmatics, the Trinity is not an afterthought or a dubious piece of theology which is tagged on to Christian belief, it is 'our thinking out the meaning of who we know the living God to be in his revelation and what in consequence we do in the Church and the World'.[9] The Trinity is the God whom we worship and Christian practice needs to be consistent with this God.

Today, we tend to use the doctrine of the Trinity in the creeds without considering its meaning or implications and without relating it to our daily lives and spirituality. As a result, our references to the different persons of the Trinity can become confused and inconsistent. The present understanding of the doctrine of the Trinity within the Church seems to indicate it to be an idea which is difficult to comprehend and which has little if any pastoral use. This may be part of the reason why the word 'God' tends to evoke an image of God as a 'Father-like' figure, rather than making one think of God as the Holy Trinity. Vincent Donovan has noted that the language which we use to describe the Trinity, such as personhood, nature, substance and being, can compromise its ongoing revelatory power to mankind because this is not the sort of language which is readily understood.[10] This may be true, but it does not mean that we can dispense with the Trinity, we rather have to reconsider how to express it for the present day. In particular we have to try to examine how the Trinity can be used to create an answer to the many contemporary problems which our world and society face. In the words of Alistair McFadyen, if we believe in God the Holy Trinity then our doctrines of Creation and Redemption must be thoroughly trinitarian.[11]

It can be argued that there is nothing new in any of the above. Mediaeval Scholastic Theology produced philosophical proofs for the existence of God, but was unable to do so for the Trinity because this was understood as a truth of revelation rather than of reason. As a result, theological discussion always began with the One God rather than with the Triune nature of that God. Whilst this may have been unavoidable, it can be argued that it reinforced the image of an unmovable and remote God and had the potential effect of removing divinity from Christ and reducing Him to the moral example of Jesus the man.

The reformed tradition of the seventeenth to nineteenth centuries suffered similar problems with the Trinity as its adherents sought to derive its dogmatics solely from scripture. This led to the rise of unitarianism, as the link of the three persons to the unity of the one God was inadequate. The best that could be hoped for here was a form of modalism – three expressions of the one undifferentiated deity. God was seen as easier to understand without the doctrine of the Trinity and so the doctrine fell into disuse.

More recently, the arguments against a 'realist' faith have also tended to dispense with the idea of God as Trinity. In 1957 Maurice Wiles dismissed the notion of Trinity, which he saw as being based on a false interpretation of the biblical accounts of Jesus and the giving of the Holy Spirit.[12] For

Wiles the best we could hope for was the division between seen and unseen God – a binitarian view. Wiles also claimed that we must never start with the Trinity and see if God will fit the mould, but rather that we must start with God and see if He must be Trinitarian. For Wiles the Trinity resulted from an 'arbitrary analysis' of the available data. It is notable that once we dispense with the doctrine of the Trinity, it becomes easier to dispense with the divinity of Christ and to see Jesus merely as an inspired human being.

The position advocated by Wiles (in which he is by no means unique) illustrates a number of the pervasive ideas which have permeated much of recent theology and which are or can become quite dangerously misleading. Starting with God and then determining whether He is trinitarian (the unitary model) is based upon the assumption of the existence of the one God. This is not the opposite of assuming the Trinity and seeing if God can be made to fit. The real alternative to the unitary model is to start with a divine threeness and then see if this can also be a divine oneness. From a philosophical stand-point, since we cannot prove the existence of God, the approach which assumes a divine threeness is no more unwarranted than the approach advocated by Wiles in which there is the assumption of a divine oneness. If Christianity teaches a triune God of three-in-one and one-in-three then we should be able to start with either position and see if it leads to the other. Examining the validity of the plurality model (three-in-one) is not the same as seeing if God fits the Trinity.

David Brown has rightly attacked those theologians who dismiss arguments in support of the Divine Trinity, arguing that they are guilty of adopting a selective approach to the subject.[13] The conceptual confusion which appears to be present in the work of some theologians is not a sound rationale against the idea that God is triune. For Brown, the belief in an interventionalist God who enters into revelatory dialogue with man is a sufficient background to the acceptance of the doctrine. He argues that we should reject the unitary model and, like the Cappadocian Fathers, adopt the plurality model in which we start from God in His threeness and examine whether a oneness emerges as a consequence. The issue of what we in fact mean by this threeness is a quite separate question. When we use language such as 'one God but three persons', we should note that the present day concept of a person is much more individualistic than the idea conveyed by the Latin 'persona' or the Greek 'υποστασισ (hypostasis) during the patristic era. Both Augustine (who used a unitary model based on psychological analogies, albeit as an illustration rather than a proof) and the Cappadocian Fathers (who preferred a plurality model) denied the presence of a distinction of persons in the immanent Trinity (the Trinity in itself) with such a distinction only being manifest in its economy (its external expression).

When they attempt to overcome the problems which they face in expressing how God can be both three and one, theologians often err in one of two different directions. They either produce ideas which are subordinationalist (in which Jesus and/or the Holy Spirit are subordinate to God the Father) or else they express their ideas in terms of modalism in which the Father, Son and Holy Spirit are understood as three expressions or forms of the same thing. For example, the Canadian Jesuit Bernard Lonergan has argued that the triune God is to be understood as 'three subjects of a single, dynamic, existential consciousness'.[14]

In developing this argument, Lonergan accepted the decree of The First Vatican Council that we cannot prove that God is triune. However, he also believed that we can show that this triune nature is possible, by considering human consciousness. Unfortunately it is unclear how his description of three subjects in a single consciousness avoids the charge of modalism, as without more than one centre of consciousness it is difficult to conceive of a relationship within the Trinity.

This issue can be explored in more detail by considering the work of Karl Rahner, who was arguably the most influential Roman Catholic theologian of the twentieth century. Rahner was critical of two aspects of the way in which trinitarian theology was presented. The first of these was the way in which there often seemed to be a separation of the doctrine of the one God from that of God The Holy Trinity. The second was the way in which the Immanent and Economic descriptions of the Trinity were often held in isolation from each other. He correctly believed that the Trinity was becoming an afterthought in everyday religious belief, with the result that popular piety was being reduced to unitarianism.

In re-presenting The Trinity in a way which avoided these problems, Rahner also wanted to avoid the risk of appearing to adopt a tritheistic position. As a result he developed an understanding of The Trinity which was based on the New Testament description of God as *O θεοσ* (literally 'The God'), which he reinterpreted as signifying The Father rather than (The) God in His trinitarian totality. The Father could then be placed alongside the New Testament references to Jesus Christ and The Holy Spirit with the result that The Trinity would be demonstrated to be consistent with the New Testament. Unfortunately, this argument is inconclusive in that there are other valid interpretations of the biblical material. Moreover it also carries the risk that if *O θεοσ* is identified with God The Father, then The Son and The Holy Spirit become subordinate.

Rahner's treatment of the Immanent and Economic Trinity is also susceptible to criticism. Although it is perfectly orthodox to state that the God who reveals Himself as triune is also triune in Himself, and that He does not merely manifest Himself in three different ways, there is a problem with Rahner's dislike of the concept of three separate consciouses in the Godhead. Although he argued that the economy of the persons can yield information about the immanent Trinity, he went on to state that he disliked the notion of 'persons', preferring instead the idea of 'distinct modes of subsisting'.[15] This statement appears to imply a modalism, although Rahner has denied that this is the case.

Moltmann believes that Rahner misunderstood the concept of personhood and that his criticism and concern seem to imply that his understanding of 'three persons' was closer to what should be termed 'three individuals'.[16] Moltmann makes the point that modern philosophical studies of personhood have maintained that a personal 'I' can only exist within a relationship to a personal 'Thou'. The lack of three consciouses in Rahner's Godhead precludes this I/Thou relationship which in turn implies that love is not possible. As a result there cannot be a relationship of love between the Father and the Son in either the Economic or The Immanent Trinity. It is also difficult to understand where the Spirit fits into the model.

In defence of Rahner, both he and Lonergan claimed that each divine person is conscious of each of the other two.[17] We should also recall that Rahner's motivation was to overcome what he saw as fundamental flaws in the way in which the Trinity was discussed in neo-scholasticism. His theology was not intended as an abstract absolute, but rather to counter an heretical tendency. It is not uncommon for an argument against a particular heresy or theological misunderstanding to overstep the mark and fall prey to a different misunderstanding.

A further criticism of Rahner which may be unjustified concerns his identification of the Economic and Immanent Trinity. Here he identified the mission or purpose of each of the three persons in the Immanent Trinity with its action or procession in the Economic Trinity, examples of the latter being creation and the bestowing of grace. The criticism is then based on the implication that the Trinity could not have existed prior to creation since no action was then possible. The logical conclusion is therefore either that the Trinity has not always been, implying either subordinationism or modalism, or that the creation was a necessary action of God, as is the bestowing of grace. The necessity of both of these actions appears to contradict the idea that God has freedom of action. However, as has already been discussed in section 4.1, the idea that creation is a part of God's nature need not imply that creation was a necessary action. A similar argument should apply here both with respect to creation and to the bestowing of grace.

In contrast to these views, Karl Barth affirmed that God *is* the Trinity and used this doctrine to open the first volume of his Church Dogmatics. For Barth, the way God is in Himself is precisely the way He is in the history of Jesus Christ, His Father and their Spirit: The Revealer, The Act of Revelation and the State of Revelation. For Barth, we too often ask the question 'What is God's place in our story?', when we should actually be asking 'What is our place in God's story?' He saw this as another manifestation of human self-centredness, believing that there is a need for us to move beyond reason and rather, in faith, to acknowledge God as Trinity. Yet Barth also talked of one God with three modes of being, a position which appears to be modalism, and he rejected any notion of a triune consciousness on the basis that this would constitute tritheism. In doing this, it appears that Barth was using the doctrine of The Trinity to secure the sovereignty of God within his theology. However, in his later writings he moved on to discuss the relationships which are involved in the doctrine and the implications of these relationships.[18]

The problem which we are facing here is the same as that which was faced by the early Church Fathers, namely how a single unity or monarchia can be split sufficiently distinctly to be three and yet still be sufficiently single to avoid both tritheism and subordinationism. The tendency is usually to err on the side of the undivided monarchia, in order to avoid tritheism, with the result that justice is not done to the Trinity and our theology can appear or become unitarian. The notable exception to this rule occurred with the Cappadocian Fathers who were then accused of tritheism. Indeed, it can be argued that all attempts to use the unitary model and thus derive the triune nature of God from His unity will inevitably fail because of the resulting and inevitable modalism or subordinationism. Pannenberg is surely correct when he writes that confusions inevitably arise when we try to derive the Trinity from the person of the Father or from the unity of the divine substance.[19] If God could indeed be understood better as a single unity rather than as Trinity (as in the reformed thought of the unitarian tradition) then there would be no need for the doctrine of the Trinity and it would never have emerged and survived in the early Church. The present premise is that an understanding of the Trinity actually renders God more understandable and more relevant to the environmental context which we are currently considering. If this is the case then an alternative approach is required.

5.2 The Social Trinity

In recent years, one popular approach to the problem of how to understand the Trinity has been to postulate a social doctrine of the Trinity, which makes use of the notion of community within the Godhead. This idea is not new, for in the twelfth century, Richard of St. Victor had noted that love (a Johannine predicate for God)[20] requires a lover, a beloved person and a third person. The third person satisfies the need for someone with whom to discuss this love and with whom to engage in a different type of relationship, so that the love in the first relationship is distinct and can be known as such. This model has reappeared recently in Brian Wren's model of God as 'Lover, Beloved and Mutual Friend' (see below, section 6.2).[21] Yet as Pannenberg notes, this model sees God as persons who are participating in love, rather than as the love itself, whereas it is love itself which appears in John's definition. It is not clear in this description that we do not have three persons each of whom is subordinate to a higher principle which is love itself.[22] Moreover, the model still derives the second and third persons as consequences of the first person, so that it is not actually a plurality model.

Heribert Mühlen drew on Richard's ideas as well as on nineteenth century developments in the study of language in which it was seen that an 'I' can only be an 'I' in relation to a 'Thou', and that a 'We' constitutes another external relationship, but one which is different to that with a 'Thou'. For Mühlen, 'I-Thou' as applied to the Holy Trinity was akin to the 'Father-Son' relationship and the mutual 'We' was personified as the Holy Spirit. This is not dissimilar to Origen's argument that the Father could not be the eternal Father without there also being the eternal Son. We should also note that the 'I' could become a 'Thou', or the 'Thou' could relate to the 'We' as an 'I-Thou', and so on. However, it is not clear that the 'We' is actually a separate person in the same way as are 'I' and 'Thou'. It has more the form of a relationship and in this respect the model is again unsatisfactory.[23]

These ideas have been developed into the concept of community, noting that a community only exists by virtue of the existence of its members and that the individual members only realise their full potential as they participate in such a community. This expression is similar to that of the Cappadocian Fathers, who saw the Trinity in terms of κοινονια (koinonia), what John Zizioulas would describe as 'Being as Communion'.[24] In fact, this state of communion is reflected in the language which we use of God. When we refer to the Trinity, we say that it is three persons, not that it is three individuals. The difference here can be stated as the fact that persons can only exist in relationship – in order to know myself I need to see myself in context. In contrast, individuals need not have any relationships. In this respect, a Trinity which consisted of three individuals rather than three persons would indeed be tritheistic. The consequence of these conclusions, is that God can only fully be Himself in as much as He is community, something which is possible within the doctrine of the Trinity but not without. God has to be triune.

In the 1970s, Wolfhart Pannenberg took these ideas and used them to examine the Trinity in terms of the mutuality of relationship between the three persons. In so doing, he also included the notion that any self-differentiation in the economy of God (that is, in God as He is experienced) must also apply to the immanency of God (that is, in God as He is to Godself).[25] He noted the distinction and relationship between Jesus and the Father who mutually disclose each other, with the Holy Spirit then being the medium of the community between the two. Pannenberg understood the three 'persons' as 'centres of activity' which are linked by perichoretic activity in a network of relationships.[26] The problem with this model would appear to be that the 'Go-Between' Spirit seems to be undertaking a different form of activity to that of either the Father or the Son. The Holy Spirit here suffers similar problems to the 'We' in the linguistic approach of Heribert Mühlen.

Yet despite these reservations, perhaps the important development in all of the above is that it has led to God being seen as dynamic, in contrast to the static doctrines of Greek philosophy and mediaeval scholasticism. Eberhard Jüngel has asked whether our focusing on God 'being-for-us' (the economy) has led us to miss out on His 'being-in-and-for-Himself' (the immanency).[27] Jüngel concluded that the whole notion of economy and immanency is a misleading result of the use of Aristotelian language of substance, which misses the point that God is dynamic in Himself and that 'God's Being is God's Becoming', as in the meaning of YHWH. Drawing on German work of the nineteenth century, Pannenberg and Rahner have also noted that the revelation of the Trinity has to be inseparable from the essential Trinity – God reveals Himself as He is eternally.[28] God is what He is and will be what He will be. The Father, The Son and The Holy Spirit become ever more united just as they become ever more distinct. It is only in their becoming united that they become distinct and only in their ongoing mutual self-distinction that they are forever becoming one.

More recently, Pannenberg has drawn out the idea that the Trinity is based on the mutual self-distinction of the persons, as in the distinction of Jesus the Son from the Father in chapters 14 to 17 of John's Gospel.[29] This mutual self-distinction rules out any possibility of different modes of being or expression (modalism) and implies instead different centres of action. Also, because the Trinity is rooted in mutual self-distinction, it rules out any discussion of the persons based solely on their origins. The expression of the Trinity is thus a whole nexus of relationships which is constitutive not only for their distinction but also for their deity.[30]

Because of this differentiation based upon relationship, the three persons cannot be added up in the sense that their sum would be any greater than one person (q.v. Augustine, De Trinitate, 6.7.9). The very way in which there is one God is tied into this relationship. When Jesus refers to the Father as the only God, this is not to deny His own deity, as it is only for the Son that this statement is true, because only He has this particular relationship. Both the differentiation and the unity of the triune God is shown by this relationship.[31] For similar reasons we should be beware of identifying the God of the Old Testament with the First person of the Trinity (God the Father), because God the Father only became known to us through His relationship with the Son. It is surely better to identify YHWH, the God of the Old Testament, the God who will be what He will be, with the undifferentiated Trinity. Biblical references to YHWH as Father are simply human descriptions of God, albeit descriptions which carried over into the early Church and which would have contributed to the use of this expression for the first person of the Trinity (see further section 6.2 below). Tom Wright has noted that if the God of whom we read in the Old Testament were to become human, then we would expect Him to be very much like Jesus of Nazareth.[32]

Both Moltmann and Jüngel have also drawn on the idea of God being love and noted the willingness of love to suffer for and on behalf of others. They ask how we can believe in a God who is apathetic. This approach could be criticised as being akin to sabellianism or patripassionism, although this would be to miss the point which they are trying to make. The original sabellian heresy (named after the early third century theologian Sabellius) was a form of modalism and was based on the idea that if Jesus suffered and the Father also suffered as a result, then they could not be two persons. The idea that God could suffer was not intrinsically heretical in itself but was seen as such because of the platonic idea of deity as a transcendent impersonal concept. Such a god is quite unlike the Christian (or Jewish) idea of the God who acts in History. Hans Urs von Balthasar noted that God could only become incarnate, die and rise (and remain God) if God is trinitarian. God the Father causes God the Son to enter abandonment and accompanies Him through God the Holy Spirit. As Moltmann notes, the suffering has to penetrate to the heart of the Trinity – The Holy Trinity has a cross at its centre. The Cross shows us the Trinity and can only be understood by an understanding of the Trinity. An adequate understanding of God the Holy Trinity has to be via the plurality model.

For Moltmann, a God who is cross centred must suffer. He believes that we have to dispense with the notion that God cannot suffer once and for all, for if God cannot suffer then neither can He love.[33] True love gives of itself and spends itself for the other. How can people respond to a god who claims to love them but does not share in their sufferings, a god who is so far off that he does not care? Such a god would fit the popular conception of God which we noted in chapter two. Of course, we should also note that when we talk of the love of God or of His suffering then we must recall that these terms are metaphorical in that we are again using human language to express something which is beyond us. They are the best we can do and the actual nature of the love and the suffering of God will be in some way different to the way in which we know them.

It is important to note in this context that the idea of a suffering God is not new. Within the Christian tradition, it was expressed anonymously during the nineteenth century and re-emerged in the early years of the twentieth century, especially in the writings of Gerald Studdert-Kennedy.[34] Moltmann has observed God's perfect freedom within this suffering, noting that God does not suffer with the creation through necessity, inevitability or inherent weakness, but simply because He is God and this is the way He has caused things to be. It is the perfect love of God, working for the good of everything to which it is directed, which leads to His suffering.

These arguments should not be interpreted as leading to a god who is weak or whose divinity and power is in any way diminished. Any worries which we may have about the idea of divine suffering should be laid to rest by a robust doctrine of the Trinity. The neglect of this doctrine in popular Christian thought is the most likely reason why the Christian faith is often seen as irrelevant, especially in times of environmental crisis. The doctrine is linked directly to the issue of God acting in the creation and to the issue of salvation. It can also help us to reconcile the idea of the God of love with the evil which we encounter in the world every day. The doctrine of the Trinity is in all probability the only Christian form of theodicy which can come anywhere near to providing a convincing answer to the question of suffering. This is the outworking not simply of Christ hanging on the cross and his resurrection, but the setting of the crucifixion and resurrection in the context of the triune nature of God. It is not possible to reconcile belief in a unitarian God with what we experience in the world. Only a triune God is believable.

5.3 The Trinity and The Crisis

So far we have only dealt a little with the way in which the Trinity itself relates to the present crisis and the way in which the Christian doctrine of the triune God is, in itself, an impor-tant element within this context. We must now consider the relevance of the Trinity in itself and the way in which it is the answer to the questions which arise out of our present envi-ronmental context. We have to do this both from the human perspective and in relation to the creation as a whole.

A fruitful approach to this subject, is to adopt the ideas of Moltmann in which he related the Trinity to the Kingdom of God and to the concept of freedom.[35] These will then provide us with the tools and insight with which we can make the connections we need. In adopting this approach, we should also recall the earlier discussions in which we noted that human freedom is related to the open nature of the universe in which we live and that the same factors which allow human freedom also permit evil and decay.

Moltmann notes the way in which the misunderstanding of God as a single monarchia, in which the Son and the Spirit are either subservient to or undifferentiated from the Father, can be related to a political system in which there is a single and all-powerful ruler.[36] This relationship is similar to the apologetic adopted by the early Church Fathers who had to demonstrate that Christians did worship a single God and did not have beliefs which were at odds with the Roman Empire and its single emperor. The logical extension of this early apologetic thought was to regard the emperor as the visible image of the invisible God which later led to the emergence of the idea of the divine rights of Kings.[37]

Whilst such thoughts are compatible with the view of God as a single undivided monarchia, or indeed with a Trinity which is subordinationalist or modalistic and therefore still has one supreme ruler, they are not compatible with a truly Trinitarian God. It is important to note that human freedom would be impossible with a monarchical tyrant of a God, for we would always have to be doing His commands. The sad fact is, that God has often come to be portrayed in this way. This is not to say that the political system of a single ruler is either correct or incorrect, but only that it does not follow as a logical consequence of a belief in God the Holy Trinity. For Moltmann, the doctrine of the Trinity is the true theological doctrine of freedom. The Glory of God is not only that of a Heavenly ruler throned in splendour, but also that of Christ on the cross and the divine creation which is indwelt by the Holy Spirit.[38]

In relating the above ideas to those of freedom and the Kingdom of God, Moltmann drew on the work of Joachim of Fiore, the twelfth century writer and mystic. Joachim is commonly seen as having identified three eras or Kingdoms in human history, namely the Kingdom of the Father, the Kingdom of the Son and the Kingdom of the Holy Spirit.[39] These Kingdoms can be seen as parallelling the ideas which are present in Luke-Acts.[40] The apparent problem with Joachim's doctrine is that his three eras appear to fail in the task of ushering in the consummation of the Kingdom of God at the end of time. The present Kingdom of the Spirit appears to be without end and as a result there is no eschaton. This was a part of the reason why Joachim was condemned by the Lateran Council in 1215.

Perhaps Joachim's real error was to separate the three persons of the Trinity and to relate each to a different era. This would not be a problem if the nomenclature was merely telling us something about each of these eras, but it does become a problem if there is a positive identification with each era, with the implication that this is the only way in which God can operate at each time. Not only would this be an expression of modalism but it would also fail to take into account the way in which the three persons can only be known in relationship and that the God of the Old Testament is not God the Father. As Pannenberg notes, the Trinity is God Himself relating to historical revelation in such a way that creation also participates in the relationship of the trinitarian persons.[41]

It is undoubtedly true that in human terms, the Holy Trinity will only be understood fully once we move beyond history and in this respect it is important to note Moltmann's belief that Joachim actually referred to four eras. The first three of these were Historical and were those referred to above. Moltmann describes these as corresponding to the creation of a world which was open to the future (an open system again); the liberation from the consequences of sin in the death of the Son, which points to future glory; and the gift of energy in the Holy Spirit as an anticipation of the eschatological dwelling in the glory of God. The fourth era was thought of as being beyond history and would be the consummation of that history (which consists of the three earlier kingdoms) in the triune Kingdom of glory.[42] Moltmann's argument is sound, for if we believe that God is triune, then the Kingdom of God which will be ushered in at the eschaton will not be the Kingdom of one single person but rather be the Kingdom of God the Holy Trinity. Indeed, this will also be the consummation of the Trinity itself, with the final ending of the negative consequences of freedom. It will be the final demonstration of the divinity of God. Because it will be the Kingdom of God the Holy Trinity, then it will be characterised by that Trinity, as will be any foretaste which we receive at the present time. This implies that any human striving to do God's will by modelling our human systems on His rule should be guided by the way in which the Kingdom is that of God the Holy Trinity. For Moltmann, the primary characteristic of this kingdom is that of freedom; the freedom which is guaranteed by the God who is not a single monarchia.

Moltmann notes that the first movement towards human freedom occurred when the human race developed the scientific and technological tools which enabled it to conquer and subdue nature rather than itself being subject to these forces.[43] Yet the power which enables this freedom can be used for good or for bad. When it is used for bad, and to exploit things or people which have no such power, overall freedom is limited because only those who have power are in possession of freedom. Everything which is subjugated to such technical power, however primitive that power may be, is denied the freedom which those with power enjoy. Power which works for good can be described as that power which has a passion for the future, with all its possibilities, and wills a similar freedom for the whole of creation. This is the way in which power is exercised by God the Holy Trinity in His giving freedom to His creation through the making of open systems. Wesley Carr has noted how the crucified God shows a divine willingness to be used and to accept the consequences of the freedom which is a part of the universe which He has created.[44] We are responsible for our actions, but God accepts responsibility for creating the freedom which makes them possible. God does not cheat by intervening and circumventing freedom whenever things go wrong. God instead has to 'stand and watch' enduring the pain as the God who was crucified.

The making of man in the image of God is God's statement that we should share in this freedom, which we are then called on to share with the rest of creation. Our use of power not for freedom, but for subjugation (whether it be of people, animals, plants or things) is a manifestation of the Sin which we examined in chapter two. This Sin was characterised by concupiscence; that state which was identified as a rejection of God and a drawing of all power to oneself for personal gain.

This relationship between freedom and the cross has a further consequence. If the environment is saved from human destruction and attains a greater degree of freedom in the world, what then should be done within this new found freedom. Should this freedom be achieved through burdening the human race with harsh penalties to protect the environment, or should humanity share in the new found freedom and joy of a creation which has been redeemed? Only if the latter is the case, and the whole nature of the relationship is transformed, will there be an affirmation of the resurrection as evidenced by a transformation in the nature of the body. Only in this latter case will humanity share this new-found freedom. This can only be the case if humanity cares for the environment without the need for legislation. The transformed nature which is achieved retains the goodness of the creation, but now as a new part of the whole. It may appear foolish for the environment to welcome its former predator, but in the Christian terms which we are using, then to do so is none other than what St. Paul described as the foolishness of God and the folly of the cross.[45]

Ultimately, true freedom will only be realised in the eschaton and the theological concept of freedom can therefore be identified with the view that the trinitarian history of God will achieve its final consummation in the trinitarian Kingdom of God. Complete freedom of the creation will only be achieved by participation in the triune God, and by the participation of the whole creation. This is what we find in Paul's writings on the removal of bonds and subjugation and the granting of freedom.

'I consider that the sufferings of this present time are not worth comparing with the glory that is to be revealed to us. For the creation waits with eager longing for the revealing of the sons of God; for the creation was subjected to futility, not of its own will but by the will of him who subjected it in hope; because the creation itself will be set free from its bondage to decay and obtain the glorious liberty of the children of God.' (Romans Ch.8 vv18-21, RSV.)

True freedom is the final gift of the triune God at the realisation of His Kingdom. It is attained only through our closeness to His presence, a closeness which we can never attain in this world. Perhaps the nearest which can be attained here is that state of spiritual union with God which has been the theme of Christian mystics of all ages. The decline in the awareness of this mystical tradition and its absence from the worship, practices and teachings of much of Western Christianity has resulted in a similar decline in the insight which this tradition can provide. It is possible that the loss of this tradition in popular piety is part of the reason for the rise of New-Age religions and pantheism. These beliefs have grown in popularity because the Christian Church has failed to meet certain human needs, both through a lack of understanding of its own doctrines and through a lack of application of its mystical tradition.

Indeed, the Church has become inarticulate in its talking about God. Not only has it largely neglected to articulate the Trinity and other elements of its rich tradition, but it has also misunderstood the meaning of religious language. As a result it misinterprets what theologians have said and are saying about God as they attempt to speak of Him in the present day using language which relates to current human experience. For this reason it is important that we examine the meaning of the language which we use of God. We need to consider what this language can tell us of the way in which we understand God and the response which this understanding allows us to make to the current environmental problems.

Notes

1. Such thinking includes works by Moltmann (1981), (1991), Pannenberg (1991), Gunton (1991) and the report 'The Forgotten Trinity', from the British Council of Churches (1989).
2. J. Thompson p.351.
3. The work and persons of The Cappadocian Fathers are discussed by

Anthony Meredith in his book 'The Cappadocians', which appears to be the only book in the English Language devoted exclusively to this subject.

4. A good overview of the development of thinking on the Trinity has been given by Pannenberg in pages 259 to 336 of the first volume of his systematic theology: Pannenberg (1991).

5. Gregory Nazianzus, Oration 27.10.

6. The most convenient English translation is on pages 62 to 64 of Stevenson (1987).

7. Moltmann (1981) pp.151ff.

8. For example, Moltmann (1991) pp.81f.

9. J.Thompson p.352.

10. Donovan (1989) p.96.

11. McFadyen (1992) pp.13–14.

12. Wiles (1957).

13. In his discussion, Brown presents a philosophical approach to the doctrine of the Trinity in which he supports an approach based on the plurality model.

14. See the review by Maynell in pp.205–216 of Ford.

15. K.Rahner (1979) pp.255ff.

16. Moltmann (1981) pp.144f.

17. Pannenberg (1991) pp.319f.

18. Moltmann (1981) pp.144f.

19. Pannenberg (1991) p.299.

20. I John Ch.4 v8.

21. Wren pp.208ff.

22. Pannenberg (1991) p.296.

23. For a discussion of Mühlen's ideas, see Pannenberg (1991) pp.430f, and Moltmann (1981).

24. Zizioulas has used this phrase as a title for a book.

25. The development of Pannenberg's ideas are reviewed by Schwöbel on pp.257ff of Ford. See also Pannenberg (1991) pp.259ff.

26. The idea of perichoresis apparently originated with John of Damascus in the eighth century; see Moltmann (1981) p.174.

27. For a discussion of the ideas of Jüngel, see the review by Webster on pp.92–106 of Ford.

28. See Pannenberg (1991) pp.300, 307 and K.Rahner (1966) pp.94ff.

29. Pannenberg (1991) pp.309ff.

30. Pannenberg (1991) pp.319–323.

31. Pannenberg (1991) p.335.

32. Wright, p.52.

33. Moltmann (1981) pp.59f. Moltmann discusses the passion of God on pp.21–60 of the same work.

34. The ideas of Studdert-Kennedy are best known through his book 'The Hardest Part' which was written in the trenches during the 1914–18 war.
35. Moltmann (1981) pp.191ff.
36. Moltmann (1981) p.192.
37. Moltmann (1981) pp.192–200.
38. Moltmann appears to reject entirely the glory of God who is enthroned in splendour and identify it totally with the crucified Christ. There is a need for a wider perspective, so that the glory of God is perceived wherever we are in His presence.
39. Moltmann (1981) pp.203ff.
40. See, for example, the discussion by Christopher Evans pp.52f.
41. Pannenberg (1991) pp.327f.
42. Moltmann (1981) p.207.
43. Moltmann (1981) pp.213ff.
44. Carr pp.134ff.
45. I Corinthians Ch.1 vv20–25.

Chapter 6

Talking about God

The doctrine of The Trinity is central to the Christian Faith and to its understanding of God. However, one of the problems which is encountered when using the doctrine is that its language of Father, Son and Holy Spirit can be so familiar that it ceases to be evocative. Indeed, this language can also carry with it a number of implicit assumptions about God which may be prejudicial to its application in the current context. This problem has resulted in the development of a number of other ways of talking about the Trinity. Some of these ideas can be helpful and offer insights into God which are not present in the traditional language. However, they must be used with caution since they could also carry implications which run contrary to mainstream understanding of the Christian Faith.

It is important that these developments in religious language are examined. If they can offer important insights into God in the present context then they are valuable. If they can mislead and present a distorted picture then we need to be aware of this problem. However, before they can be considered in this way, we need to discuss in more detail the way in which we understand religious language and what this language actually means. We can then move on to examine some of the alternative ways of referring to God which have emerged in recent years.

6.1 The Language Which We Use of God

Whenever we write or talk about God, we do so in human language, using human expressions. We rarely stop to ask

ourselves how adequate these expressions are as a description
of the God to whom they are supposed to refer. This language
which we use is important, not only because it may express
something of who or what we believe God to be, but also
because it can shape our feelings and emotions about God, as
well as influencing the way in which we come to think about
Him.[1] Our unwitting, but repeated use of particular language
has the power to change our beliefs. If we repeatedly use a
particular description, then we eventually come to see this
description as being correct, irrespective of its original validity
or status.

The descriptions of God which we use are drawn from a
variety of sources, some of them traditional or scriptural,
others originating in contemporary thought. In describing or
naming God in this way, it is important to realise that since
God is far more than the World, any single human name or
description is inadequate to express the totality of God's being.
In addition, we should remember Arthur Peacocke's observation that the descriptions which we use for God cannot be
verified in the same way as is often possible with their scientific counterparts.[2] We cannot put God under a microscope to
see if He matches the words which we use about Him. The
hymn writer and theologian Brian Wren has noted the danger
which exists when name God untruthfully, as this results in us
deluding ourselves and to the worship of an idol rather than the
true God.[3]

Thomas Aquinas drew attention to this problem in question
13 of volume 1a of his 'Summa Theologica' where he
concluded that there is a balance to be achieved between saying
that human language can be used of God and saying that it
cannot. He noted, for instance, that verbs and actions both
assume the existence of time, but that God is beyond time, and
that nouns assume either a concrete or an abstract nature, but
that God is neither. As a result, when we apply human
language to God, we have to adopt what we could term a
linguistic shift. Ian Ramsey drew on this distinction between
describing what God does and what God is (verbal and logical
statements, respectively), noting that we should not confuse
the two types of statement and that we are on much more
certain ground when we use the former.[4] We experience God

through His actions rather than as He is in His absolute Being. Aquinas qualified his statements about God with the conclusion that 'This is what is ultimate in the human knowledge of God: to know that we do not know God.' When we use human language of God we should remember that the words which we use do not bear exactly the same meanings as when we apply them to the creation. In religion, everyday language is used to point beyond itself to that which is ultimate.

One consequence of the fact that our descriptions and names for God are formulated in human terms is that these descriptions make use of metaphors. The use of metaphor and its consequences in religious language have been discussed in detail by Janet Martin Soskice.[5] Soskice makes the important point that metaphorical language is often poorly understood and that as a result such language is sometimes seen as diminishing the truth about God rather than allowing us to refer to God in language which can be understood. Ramsey alluded to this latter point when he noted that theological articulacy is achieved by the use of models of God: what Francis Bacon had seen as saying the unsayable to know the unknowable.[6]

Soskice has defined a metaphor as, 'That figure of speech whereby we speak about one thing in terms which are seen to be suggestive of another'.[7] If we accept this definition, then we can see a metaphor as being the intersection of two ideas: the subject under discussion, usually referred to as the primary idea or tenor, and the idea which illuminates it, usually referred to as the secondary idea or vehicle. As an example, in the statement 'The clouds were cotton-wool', clouds is the tenor and cotton-wool the vehicle. Although no explicit reference need be made to the tenor, both tenor and vehicle together form the metaphor, not simply the vehicle taken in isolation.

It is important to realise that although a metaphorical statement informs us about the tenor, it is not making a literal statement about that tenor. When we use a metaphor we are actually stating that there is a scale of meaning which relates the tenor to the vehicle. In our example above, the clouds are not to be understood literally as cotton-wool, but there is something about cotton-wool which helps us grasp the appearance of the clouds if we have not seen them. When we use a metaphor to talk about God then we are doing a similar thing. This is what Paul Tillich described as the difference between Symbol God and God as Being.[8] We need to distinguish between God as we are able to describe Him given the limitations of human expression (Symbol God) and God as Godself.

Soskice notes that a true metaphor does not exist for its own sake, as a substitution for literal speech, but in order to say something which can be said in no other way. Both the intention of the speaker and the interpretation of the listener are therefore important. The meaning of the metaphor will depend on its context, both linguistically and otherwise. Soskice is quick to dismiss questions such as 'What is x a metaphor for?', because they miss the point that if we could answer such a question then we would not need the metaphor at all. Such questions also illustrate the mistake of seeing 'x' as the metaphor, whereas the true metaphor is the whole statement which contains 'x'. We can illustrate this by the use of an example. The metaphorical statement 'I am a child in my mother's arms', when made by an adult in a religious context, is not necessarily likening the adult to a child nor is it stating that God is a mother or claiming that God has arms. The metaphor, as the whole statement, is saying something about the relationship between the believer and that in which he or she believes. It achieves this by referring to one thing in terms which are suggestive of another.

It should therefore be realised that if we consider a metaphor as a literal statement, then it is always false. Clouds are not cotton wool; the adult is not a child in its mother's arms. Yet through its scale of meaning a metaphor does convey a truth even though it is, itself, literally a false statement. It is therefore erroneous to claim, as Brian Wren does, that metaphors of God say both something of what God is and something of what God is not. A metaphor is not apophatic for it does not seek to conceal God, nor does the use of one particular metaphor preclude us from making any other metaphorical statement about God. A metaphor rather says something new about God, something which could be said in no other way, as the language which we use refers to more than what is and articulates the possible. Perhaps this is what we should expect when we use language to refer to the God who has disclosed Himself as *YHWH* – I will be what I will be.

We should therefore avoid terminology such as 'mere metaphor' and 'only a metaphor', for such phrases not only miss the point of what metaphorical speech is about, but they also fail to recognise that the whole sentence and its context forms the metaphor. A theologian who claims to write metaphorically and has the understanding of metaphor outlined above is in no way diminishing the truth. When Vincent Donovan criticises traditional religious language, he fails to realise that what is required is not a new theology for new people but rather the re-expression of old metaphors which no longer speak to such people in the form of new metaphors which speak the truth in a way which is relevant to them.[9] The problem then is how to know that the new metaphors convey the same truth as the old, albeit that different people will understand the truth contained in the traditional metaphors in different ways. We have to resist the temptation to take heed of those who call for the reduction of religious metaphors to literal truth and who criticise such metaphors if they are non-reducible. By the very nature of a metaphor such a reduction is not possible and those people who call for such a reduction do not understand what they are asking.

A metaphor can clearly tell us something new about God. In addition, beyond the metaphor and its scale of meaning will lie a model which it may or may not be useful to explore and to develop. However, if we find that there are many points of correspondence between the tenor and the vehicle of our metaphor, and that its scale of meaning continues to produce further insights into the nature of God beyond its original intention, then it becomes valid to extract the vehicle and treat it as a model.[10] This model will bear some form of direct relationship with that which it represents and it is valid to ask what information or insight we can gain from each and every facet of the model. Even so, we must again be beware of a false literalism. There will be a limit to the relationship between the model and the real thing or prototype.

Models also play an important role in science and there has been much debate about the similarities between the roles of models in science and in theology and whether the two types of model are actually the same. This is an issue which has been discussed by Ian Barbour in his book 'Theology in an Age of Science'.[11] Such comparison of religious models with scientific models can cause problems when this comparison is made by those whose experience is limited to only one of these two fields of study. Soskice, for example, notes two distinctions which have been drawn between scientific and religious models and whilst she criticises one of these distinctions, the present contention is that they are both erroneous. The first distinction states that scientific models are structural and causal, whereas religious models are evocative and affective. The second is that there is a contrast between the use of models as scientific aids to theorizing, in which models are actually dispensable mathematical tools which can be replaced by the real thing, and religious models where the model can only be replaced by another model.

Soskice notes that the first distinction misses the point that religious models are used as aids to explanation and to help us understand concepts such as the Trinity. Such a use is both structural and causal as well as evocative and affective. The present contention is that although Soskice is correct, it is also true that the better scientific models bear the potential to be evocative and affective for they can display beauty through their symmetry and expression.

The second distinction fails to understand modern science, for it misses the point that all scientific theories have the nature of models and that not all such models are subservient to mathematics.[12] Whilst Classical Realism did carry the assumption that scientific models and theories were literal descriptions of the world, it is now usually accepted that this position is erroneous (see, for example, the discussion by Barbour).[13] Like their religious counterparts, scientific models are subject to much debate and are not always open to experimental verification. They are neither exact descriptions of the World, as in Classical Realism, nor are they simply calculating tools devoid of reality, as in Instrumentalism. In both science and religion we can see simple models parallelled by more complex mathematical and linguistic expressions, where the simple and the complex are mutually illuminating. As Ramsey notes, all models fail when they are pushed to their limits.[14]

No single model (or metaphor) is adequate and the best religious language is that which is consistent with the largest number of separate models.

It is the present contention that in both science and religion, models are based on the idea of Critical Realism. This is the concept that things exist prior to the construction of human models and that the models which we construct are always incomplete. In both science and theology, a given understanding of the world or of God will embrace a number of complementary models. As an example, scientists use two different models to describe light. In one model light is described in terms of waves and in the other in terms of particles. In Christian Theology we construct different models for God and He is portrayed, for example, both as a shepherd and as a Father.

There still remains the question of how we choose between different models (the question of preference) and how we can test whether they are actually talking of God (the question of reference). Although his approach has been criticised, Ramsey postulates two tests which we should apply to our models of God.[15] First, they must be able to co-exist with other models and the set of models has to have some overall degree of self-consistency. Secondly, the resulting 'multi-model disclosure' must fit the universe; as Polkinghorne has put it, it must be consistent with 'the way the world is'.[16] This second test prevents a plethora of similar but erroneous models taking over by sheer weight of numbers. As an aside we might note that this is the same general procedure which is often used in verifying scientific models of atmospheric chemistry such as those used to examine the consequences of atmospheric pollution. It is important to note that this approach does not prove a model, it simply helps us to see that it is not nonsensical. The task in the earlier chapters of the present work has been to show that traditional Christian doctrine provides models which are tenable in the context of an environmental crisis.

Moltmann describes religious symbols and metaphors as representing the tension which exists between experience and religious expression.[17] This is akin to what the North-American feminist theologian Sallie McFague describes as the use of metaphor to express the inexpressible.[18] We only use metaphors and models to describe God because we have no alternative; without them there is nothing that we could say. There is therefore value in exploring the use of different metaphors and models to express our understanding of God. This can result in a move towards what Song has described as the use of artistry and intuition in oriental thought to move in regions which are inaccessible to human logic.[19] It also addresses the problem identified by McFague, in which modern theology has attempted to deconstruct and demythologise traditional Christian images, but has undertaken little reconstruction work to replace them with something which is potentially more accurate and relevant.[20] Of course, if the language associated with these traditional images is metaphorical then it can be argued that such demythologisation is not possible anyway.

These two points of Song and McFague are also important if we are to produce a theology which is able to partake of dialogue with Christian spirituality rather than being simply a cerebral exercise. Spirituality exists beyond the purely cerebral and also expresses the essence of emotions and relationships. If it can inform our theology then this is for the good, especially as a particular theology should not exist in isolation but rather both feed and be fed by the worshipping community of the religion concerned. This implies that although McFague's point concerning theological reconstruction is valid, any images or symbols which we use cannot be imposed upon a worshipping community. Instead they have to emerge from within that community; they have to be tried and tested from within the faith. This view is consistent with F.W. Dillistone's distinction between signs and symbols, in which a sign can be imposed and is immediately recognisable by people who see it, whereas a symbol emerges from within a tradition and cannot be imposed from the outside.[21]

However, if we are to examine the images which we use for God and to say something which can re-express old truths for a modern age, then we still need to ground our images somewhere. We need to portray the familiar in a novel way, and yet not produce something which is totally unfamiliar. As Gregory of Nazianzus noted:

'The one who makes the best theologian is not the one who knows the whole truth, for the chain of the flesh is incapable of receiving the whole truth, but the one who creates the best picture.'[22]

For Gregory, as for the other Cappadocian Fathers (Gregory of Nyssa and Basil of Caesaria), such a picture of God would certainly have been trinitarian for they were staunch defenders of the doctrine of The Trinity. Our picture of God must also be trinitarian and any model which does not meet this criterion must be rejected as contrary to the Christian faith. With this criterion in mind we can now move on to examine the way in which models for God have been suggested and used, and the ways in which these models might inform us about the Trinity.

6.2 Models for God

The obvious way to examine the development of divine models is to begin with the two principal sources of Christian Theology, namely the Bible and tradition. However, if we are to work in a way which is relevant to the present day we should not ignore the additional influences of reason, culture and experience. Nor should we overlook revelation, for to do so would be to deny or ignore the work of the Holy Spirit. Yet it is important that we do not 'invent' models at will, just because they happen to sound good or look interesting. We need rather to draw on the rich treasury of images which are present within our Christian heritage, whether tradition or scripture, and to examine their relevance to the context which is under consideration.

There is also a second caution which we should heed, this time relating to the nature of metaphors. Although we need to affirm the importance of metaphors in our methodology, we also need to be aware that the relationship between metaphorical language and the Bible can result in what Sallie McFague terms the twin problems of biblical fundamentalism. On the one hand we can fail to see that the theology is metaphorical and can therefore take all biblical descriptions as being literally true, and yet on the other hand we can also fail to see that there is truth both within and beyond that which is expressed in each metaphor.[23] Each metaphor contains a statement of the truth, but does not necessarily exhaust that truth. We need to remind ourselves of the danger in using expressions such as only a metaphor'.

A manifestation of this approach to the Bible is what Brian Wren describes as 'Patriarchal Fundamentalism', which he sees as being either a gift given for us to enjoy, or 'one of the oldest, deepest, and most pervasive sins we know'.[24] This is an important claim, for in chapters two and three of the present work we have already noted the problems which can be caused by regarding God as wholly transcendent. However, Wren overstates his case, because in speaking of God's transcendence, the patriarchal model is valuable, and the problem lies in its overemphasis rather than in its absolute inappropriateness. We would also do well to recall that its original purpose was to make God seem closer to people on earth rather than to keep Him at a distance. Moltmann has again drawn attention to the work of Studdert Kennedy, in which he noted the suffering, the sorrow and the loving aspects of fatherhood, asking where these are in the patriarchal models which we use for God.[25] Fatherhood should speak of immanence as well as of transcendence and lead us to reflect on the closeness of our relationship with God. There is also the feminist critique to consider, in which the word 'Father' is seen as sexist in its application to God. However, even if God is the absolute ideal father, then in as much as this model speaks to us via our experience of human fathers it has to be incomplete due to the imperfection in these human figures.

Pannenberg has noted that the term 'Father' was used to refer to God in the Old Testament before its use in a personal sense by Jesus and he has related this usage to its original context.[26] It seems that unlike some pagan cults, the Israelites did not see the term 'Father' as implying sexual differentiation within their God (YHWH) and thereby avoided the further conclusion in which such differentiation was usually taken as implying polytheism. The term 'Father' was a non-sexual expression of their relationship with YHWH rather than a description of the head of a group of polytheistic gods. This came to be an important distinction from other Near Middle-

Eastern religions. At a later date the descriptive and relational term 'Father' came to be used as a proper name for God. This is what may lie behind the confusion in early Christian apologetics in which the word 'Father' could sometimes refer to the first person of the Trinity and sometimes to the undivided Trinity, complete in itself. Because of these origins, we should only need to consider revising our talk of God as 'Father', whether from Israelite or Jewish origins or from Jesus Himself, if this description reflects only the social prejudices of the time or if it is a psychological projection – which Pannenberg claims is not the case. Indeed, Pannenberg notes that the description of God as 'Mother' is more likely to be a projection.[27]

Turning next to the monarchical model of God, McFague goes much further than Wren, and sees this model as inherently dangerous because it produces an asymmetry between us and God. She perceives a monarch as distant and remote from its subjects.[28] Yet any model for the divine which omits elements of asymmetry must surely be false since otherwise we would be made equals with God. Any description which contains such an equality must surely be suggestive of self-idolatry. Moreover, although McFague rejects the suggestion that her description of a monarch is a caricature, it is increasingly out of touch with the reality in western Europe.[29] Her criticism is also out of touch with the understanding of the Celtic tradition within Christianity. Here, the repeated references to God as Lord, King or Chief, have to be taken within the context of the Celtic understanding of a King, that is, as one who dwelt within and amongst the people and who was able to be approached by any member of the community.[30]

Both Wren and McFague have developed models of God which take account of what they perceive as the overemphasis given to a powerful transcendent God. Such models are themselves open to criticism because they are also in danger of producing an unbalanced theology. David Nicholls believes that we need to guard against what he describes as a welfare image of God, by which he seems to mean a God who sympathises with us in our suffering, but is either unable or unwilling to act.[31] This is similar to the God referred to by Epicurus which we noted in chapter 3. Nicholls believes that modern theology is losing touch with the sovereign God who acts in history. By trying to be relevant to the modern world, theology runs the risk of producing a god who reflects the characteristics of that world.

Nicholls' critique contains a great deal of truth. Although it is important to defend the insight that God allows Himself to know pain as an integral part of what it is to love and to allow freedom (see section 4.2) this cannot be allowed to become the whole picture. As a reaction against the overemphasis on the transcendent aspect of God which has occurred in the past, there now seems to be a shift towards an over-emphasis on the immanence of God. Far from working towards a solution to the environmental crisis, excessive stress on the immanence of God can lead to an expression of human dominance in the world. What began as a movement to re-express God's immanence and relationship with the whole of creation may produce a god who is little else and who is devoid of any power and glory.

It may well be true that even when we hold the transcendence and immanence of God together, we are still guilty of not letting the transcendent God be big enough. To allow Him His full transcendent majesty would place Him beyond human comprehension, and this is something we are unwilling to allow. It is paradoxical that as our perception of the size of the Universe increases, so we try to make God smaller. Perhaps it is the case that a loss of faith in the resurrection and in eschatology (see Ch.4.) and the associated loss of an eternal 'reward' produces a subconscious desire to punish God. Making God small and depriving Him of His power could be the method by which we inflict this punishment. If we allow our theology to include the insight of the God who can feel pain, we also need to safeguard the transcendent power of God within that same theology.

In constructing models of God, we need to attempt to express both the Being of God as God is in Himself and the way in which He relates to the world. In this respect Sallie McFague is right to note that if Jesus illustrates God and His relationship with the World for all time, then we have to use the insights which we find in Him which speak to our present condition.[32] Working from this premise Wren has produced three criteria against which he believes we should test our models of God. These are first that they should be strong and vivid, secondly that they should be active – expressing direction and liberation – and thirdly that they should be Trinitarian.[33] He sees the third point as particularly important and stresses that not only should our models be Trinitarian, but that they should also avoid any risk of the charge of subordinationism. He believes that this can be achieved if we express the mutual indwelling and unity of this Trinity (perichoresis).[34]

This final point implies that if each of the three names used of the three persons of the Trinity is valid, then these names can also be used adjectivally of each of the other two persons. This is a conclusion which can also be drawn from the statement of Basil of Caesaria in the fourth century that 'Everything that the Father is, is seen in the Son and everything that the Son is belongs to the Father.'[35] As an example, if we apply this idea to Brian Wren's model of the Trinity as Lover, Beloved and Mutual Friend, then it implies that the Lover is a beloved Lover and a mutually friendly Lover. In the discussion which follows, we shall examine a number of models of the Trinity which have been suggested before we select one particular model for our present context.

The first of these models, is one which is increasingly being used as a gender inclusive form of the traditional trinitarian formula. This describes God as 'Creator, Redeemer and Sustainer'. There is no doubt that these are three important and powerful descriptions of God. However, one problem with this model is that within Christian theological understanding all three persons of the Trinity are seen as creative. In the model, this creative activity is concentrated on the first person alone, even if redeeming and sustaining are understood as the ongoing creative work of God. A second problem with this model is that the use of gender inclusive language can depersonalise God. Such depersonalisation becomes a problem if the descriptions are used exclusively or on a regular basis. Susan Thisthlewaite has argued that the criterion should not be that of gender inclusive/exclusive language, but instead the concept of linguistic visibility/invisibility.[36] This means that we should not suppress any reference to gender with the intention of removing a sexual bias, but rather use both male and female metaphors, as appropriate, in our attempts to talk about God. Even if we reject this argument, it does not alter the fact that we are far more familiar with Fathers and Sons than with Creators and Redeemers. The traditional model is one which speaks to the theologically inarticulate in a way which talk of a Creator and Redeemer cannot.

This model is also flawed in that rather than considering three persons, it instead takes personalised forms of three related activities, and must therefore be considered a form of modalism. God has become three modes of action rather than three interrelated persons. Despite the fact that it can appear more ecologically friendly than traditional expressions, this model is not true to Christian doctrine. In attempting to avoid subordinationism, those who use this model make the opposite error of modalism. Contrary to the ideas of the second and third centuries, both Athanasius and the Cappadocian Fathers noted that there is no distinction between the three persons of the Trinity in terms of their action. For them the distinction in the Trinity is known by the revelation of the Son and the Holy Spirit, not by different spheres of operation. Activities should only be related to the three persons of the Trinity after we have first articulated the Trinity itself.

The second model is that suggested by Sallie McFague. In this model she describes God as 'Mother, Lover and Friend', and identifies each of the three persons with a different aspect of love, these being respectively αγαπε *(agape)*, εροσ (eros) and øιλια (philia).[37] She also qualifies the word 'Mother', by referring to it as 'Mother (and father)', making the point that for her the emphasis should be on the use of female (and male) metaphors rather than feminine and masculine ones. For McFague, the issue is one of gender and asking what the image can tell us of the divine, rather than embodying God with qualities and attributes which are thought of as feminine and masculine.[38] However, the model of 'αγαπε, εροσ and øιλια' suffers from the same problems as that of 'Creator, Redeemer and Sustainer'. Each of these three forms of love becomes identified with one person so that the distinction is again made in terms of divine activity and we have another form of modalism.

Wren also has reservations about masculine and feminine

attributes, noting that the use of female metaphors can still express the attitudes of a patriarchal society and that in these circumstances they can produce the image of a god who is weak.[39] If God is described in feminine terms to those who identify femininity with weakness and vulnerability then this can only serve to reinforce the concept of a God who is incapable of decisive action. Instead, Wren prefers to use the inclusive but highly personal metaphor of 'Lover, Beloved and Mutual Friend', in which the Third person expresses the relationship between the First and Second, as well as between the Trinity and the World.[40] The problem in this model occurs in the notion of the 'Mutual Friend'. When we consider the Mutual Friend in human terms, we will tend to form a picture of a person who is outside the core relationship and hence one who is participating in weaker relationships than that between the first two persons. This is the same problem noted in chapter five, namely that the three persons must be of equal standing. Moreover, Wren himself notes that his metaphor 'rarely occurs in human relationships',[41] and in so doing he implicitly accepts that it is a weak metaphor, for it is difficult for us to either identify with the metaphoric vehicle or to be moved by its power. It is therefore of little use in helping us to understand or talk about the God whom we worship.

If we explore the issue more widely and look at metaphors and models which may reflect only one person of the Trinity, we should note that the Spirit is pictured in the Bible as wind, fire and water/rain[42], but not as earth, the fourth of the elements in classical thought. Macquarrie links this to the desire to exclude the idea of the earth as a female deity.[43] This idea would have been experienced as the 'World Mother' in cults such as those found in Canaan, as well as the more developed idea of the 'Universal Mother Earth' (Ishtar, Diana, Isis, Gaia etc).[44] Today we need to guard against the pantheistic tendencies shown by Lovelock's Gaia hypothesis, whilst also taking note of St. Francis' reference to Mother Earth and the teachings of the Celtic tradition on the goodness of creation.

Another widespread model of God is that of God as artist, as in Hendry's description of artistry as a model for divine creativity.[45] In this model artistry is seen as the rapid expression of an idea held in the mind of the artist, which then develops gradually with time. The artist expresses himself and his intentions in his work, which nonetheless takes on a separate existence in a different medium to that of the artist. This is similar to Bill Vanstone's description of the two schoolboys building a model of a tract of countryside.[46] Biblically we also find references to God as a potter, moulding the clay.[47] Arthur Peacocke has developed these analogies to encompass the image of a bell-ringer who is continually ringing the changes and elaborating the melody.[48] However, Gerald Daly, writing on creation and redemption, points out a weakness in these models, namely that the created artifact is too highly determined by the artist. He prefers the idea of a playwright or a composer, both of whom have to let go of their creation, which then finds its expression through others who have the freedom to change it against the creator's wish.[49]

A strong biblical model which we should not overlook is that of the shepherd. This is applied both to God in the Old Testament and to Jesus in the New. Its merit is that in both sets of writings it is revealed by God as He applies it to Himself.[50] Yet it could be argued against this model that the word shepherd still has strong masculine overtones, at least in the west. Its widespread biblical usage is both a disadvantage, since it does not have the value of being a novel idea in which we can still recognise God, and an advantage in that it is a part of tradition and not a recent human invention.

A disadvantage which is shared by all the models discussed above, is that they have a tendency to emphasise the love of God. Although we should not deny this love, we need to be beware that overemphasis of this aspect of the Godhead does not lead us to lose sight of other important elements of Christian faith. We need to ensure that we do not lose sight of the Doctrine of Sin and Evil which we discussed earlier. Evil in the world is clearly visible all around us and we should not ignore this. Our doctrine of God needs to be able to cope with these facts. Similarly, we need to maintain an ethical content within our faith. The doctrine of Grace and Divine love and forgiveness should not blind us to the need to distinguish between right and wrong. There needs to be a statement of Christian ethical positions together with clear statements of why we hold these positions. Models of God as judge seem to be falling from favour and losing their impact, yet it is precisely such a model which can address the ethical issues of our time and draw attention to human failings in our role as stewards of the divine creation.

6.3 A Model for God in the Present Crisis

None of the models of God outlined above seem to be particularly relevant to the environmental context of the present day. If the Trinity is to be seen as pertinent, then it must be so in its own right as well as in the language which we use for the three persons. We need to set our horizons more widely and to produce a new model which speaks more directly to this situation. We shall do this by examining each person of the Trinity in turn.

The image of God as a gardener provides one description of the first person of the Trinity which may fit the present need. This idea has been alluded to by McFague and was used by Wren in his epilogue, although neither of them explored its consequences.[51] The idea has the advantage of being rooted firmly within the biblical tradition, whilst still being novel due to its infrequent use in the present day. In the Bible, the Yahwistic account of creation in chapter two of Genesis describes how God planted a garden in Eden. Trito-Isaiah's vision of Israel as a well watered garden also suggests this metaphor, as does the Old Testament idea of Israel as a vineyard.[52] The general concept is again present in the New Testament in Jesus' parables of the kingdom.[53] However, the most explicit reference occurs in chapter fifteen of John's Gospel, following Jesus claim to be the true vine. Here He says 'My Father is the gardener' (or 'vinedresser', depending on the translation), with the Greek γεοργοσ (georgos) being a word meaning farmer or cultivator.[54] In his commentary on John's Gospel, the German New-Testament theologian Rudolf Bultmann expressed the opinion that although the usage in this chapter could be incidental, it is more likely to have been a deliberate choice by the author, reflecting a common contemporary metaphor for God.[55]

The concept of a gardener fits in well with the description of the creative activity of God given above. A gardener is clearly a form of artist and Hendry's description of artistry as a metaphor for God's creation fits this form of work rather more closely than it fits the idea of God as a painter. Both a garden and the divine creation have separate lives of their own, and both contain within themselves the potential to be something of great beauty, whilst also being subject to decline and decay. The gardener can dwell within the garden, being immanent to it, or can leave it alone for a while, during which time he or she becomes transcendent. In addition, the gardener has to work within the garden to weed it and maintain it, whilst allowing most of the plants the freedom to develop as they will. The garden is also a place where death can occur. However, the gardener is not just a welfare figure, for there are times when vicious pruning is necessary, or when drastic action is needed to rid the garden of some form of pest. The gardener is also a gambler, who relies on chance factors, as well as a lover who bestows care on his or her creation. The ideal gardener fits the criteria of perfect love and creativity drawn up by Vanstone, which he saw as speaking of the nature of the love of God.[56] The model of God as gardener speaks to us not only of the nature of the Father, but also points to those of the Second and Third Persons and the Trinity as a whole. It may also speak to those of a non-western culture, especially if the Greek γεοργοσ is translated directly rather than via the English.

The gardener model was also used by the philosopher John Wisdom in his well-known argument concerning the existence of God.[57] John Macquarrie has noted that much of Wisdom's discussion concerns not the absence or presence of the gardener (God), but whether the plot of ground being considered actually is a garden or whether it is a wilderness.[58] In our present context this is a crucial question. If we see the world as a garden to be cared for, then this will elicit a different response to that in which we see it as a patch of wasteground for us to exploit as we will. Gardens serve a variety of purposes; some areas are used to produce food, others are developed for their beauty and others are left as a haven both for animal life and for wild plants which might otherwise not survive. Gardens which are overworked or exploited by their tenants become exhausted of nutrients and lose their beauty and capacity for new growth. The parallels to the world here are obvious, and the gardening God is unlikely to be happy with the behaviour of His tenants. We should recall that in the Yahwistic narrative (Genesis Ch.3) man was expelled from the garden because he did not abide by the rules imposed by the gardener. Jesus' parable of the tenants in the vineyard (Mark Ch.12 vv1-9) tells of similar consequences. This parable can speak directly to the situation of the present day.

Turning to the second person of the Trinity, we shall adopt the idea of God as 'Lover'. This metaphor has already been discussed in detail by McFague and Wren, with the present discussion of love in chapter 4 also illustrating this idea. McFague's Lover reflected love exclusively as ερσσ, despite the presence of αγαπε and øιλια in the other persons of her Trinity. In contrast to these ideas, the present Lover is much more all-embracing, being concerned with God as a questioning, challenging, self-giving and suffering lover. Questioning and challenging because he gives freedom and invites response, whilst at the same time asking of our motives and our aims; questioning whether our priorities and actions are in accord with his intentions for the creation. Self-giving and suffering, because He has expressed Himself in creation and because all our failures and disasters are inflicted, either directly or indirectly upon Him. God is the Lover who has taken a gamble in creation and who accepts the consequences of this freedom which He created, through His death on the cross.

The present use of the model of 'Lover' therefore contains much more of a balance between αγαπε, ερσσ and øιλια. We should note in particular the depth of feeling and relationship which is added by ερσσ, and the longevity which is contributed by øιλια. Tillich saw the unity of all forms of love as being expressed in what he called the 'urge toward the reunion of the separated'.[59] In this respect, the model of God as Lover expresses the desire for reconciliation and redemption which is a part of the Christian message, whilst also accepting the risk which is inevitable in a universe in which entropy increases. Rowan Williams has noted that if we believe in a God who communicates with us then risk is unavoidable, because communication involves risk for all involved. Without risk there could not be a communicative God.[60] Williams' words speak directly to our present context when he notes that conversation and relationships can survive risk and misunderstanding if there is sufficient time available for rebuilding. The resurrection points to God making this time available. For our environmental crisis, this is the time which a loving God has made for us to repent and to attempt to change our ways and use the world in a less exploitative manner. Yet we must avoid the old trap of relying on our own resources. There is also a need to turn back to the loving God and to call on Him to help. To quote Williams:

'Our hope cannot lie in the possibility of avoiding risk, but in the assurance that God has time to work against our self-serving, self-defining responses to God's 'Word', God's entry into our human conversation'.[61]

This recalls our discussion of the need to see both the present and the eschatological realisations of the Kingdom of God.

McFadyen notes that this aspect of communication and risk is important if the social doctrine of the Trinity and its account of personhood is to be taken seriously.[62] Identity in personhood involves communication and relationship and we have already noted how this is reflected within the triune God. The oneness of God implies that there are external relationships as well as internal relationships, and so the social doctrine bears within itself the risk implied by these external relationships. These external relationships, which are the same creation and redemption which we examined in chapter four, are borne by a God who is described as Lover. For the present argument, it is notable that creation and redemption are often assigned to the Word of God, the second person of the Trinity – that person whom we see here as the risk taking lover.

The notion of divine risk is not confined to external relationships. The death of the Son of God raises questions about the deity of God the Father, about how and why God could allow this to occur (a divine parallel to theodicy), and about what transpired within the Trinity itself. What are the implications for the Father/Son relationship if the Son is crucified? If the Father and the Son are defined within their mutual relationship (see section 5.1), then the deity of the immanent Trinity is involved with the course of events in the world. This not only questions God's deity, but also the immanent relationships within the Trinity.[63] Perhaps it is this which points to the pain which God consents to know.

Turning to the third person of the Trinity, we shall consider the idea of God as 'Dancer'. The metaphor of God the dancer is far from new and is perhaps more familiar to those from an eastern culture than to those from the west. In this respect it broadens the scope of the model and gives it an increased global perspective. In Hindu thought, God is the dancer and he therefore creates the dance. The dance, that is the creation, is different from the dancer, but also wholly dependent upon Him. If the dancer should stop dancing, then the dance ceases to exist; it cannot be separated or taken away. Moltmann notes that the idea of the world as dance is present as a mystery in many African and eastern cultures.[64] Here the dance is seen as supplying divine energies to those who participate in the ritual, transforming the dancer to share in the nature of the god depicted in the dance. The most well-known manifestation of this occurs in Shiva Nataraja, who is seen as expressing the five divine activities of creation, preservation, destruction, the giving of rest, and release and salvation.[65] There are strong parallels in these activities with the different aspects of creation which we have identified in the Christian tradition. The one which we have avoided here is that of destruction, although this is certainly found throughout the Old Testament, as well as in traditional Christian concepts of eschatology and the wrath of God.

In early Christian thought, Neoplatonism adopted the idea of dance to express the eschatological freedom of a soul released from the body. Here, the Logos was the leader of the sacred round which moved the world. Dance was also used to describe the nature of the relationship between the three Persons of the Trinity, and can be implied by the concept of perichoresis (proceeding around). If we use the model of God the Dancer to refer to the third person of The Trinity, we can attempt to recover the idea of God indwelling the whole of creation. We can rediscover the idea that nature is sacred, not because of a plethora of polytheistic deities as in nature cults, but because it is all indwelt by the one God who created it. In this way we might also recover the reverence and respect for the natural world which was held by our ancestors, and which has been preserved within the Church by the Franciscan and Celtic traditions. The God who dances in creation reinforces his statement that the creation is good.

If we take Wren's understanding of perichoresis, and interchange our models of Gardener, Lover and Dancer, then we obtain a Loving Gardener and a Dancing Gardener; a Gardening Lover and a Dancing Lover; a Gardening Dancer and a Loving Dancer. The addition of these internal qualifications serves to build the model in a way which adds substance to each of the three Persons. It is important to remember that these are metaphors and models and are in no way intended to describe the whole of the reality which is God. They are not absolutes, but are rather ideas to help us to explore the being of God and to see if their insights prove to be valuable and in accordance with our experience in the world. We have to be aware of the risk involved in metaphorical theology and of the destabilising influence its insights can have if they are used indiscriminately, unwisely, or if the model is pushed too far. An example of this in the gardener model of God might be how we are to interpret suffering in the world. This could be seen either as the action of a pest working against the gardener, or as the pruning and uprooting which is needed in order to enable the garden to grow.

Yet even when we bear these factors in mind, the present model could be criticised for being too cosy and homely, even if it does provide further insights into God. God the Gardener may open up our understanding of the First Person of the Trinity, but we all know gardeners who neglect their gardens or who are half-hearted in their efforts. The fact that similar criticisms also apply to fathers does not defend the present model. God the Lover is valid, especially when used in the qualified sense above, but 'Lover' is also ambiguous and open to widespread misinterpretation in the world today. For many Christians, God the Dancer is too suggestive of doctrines and myths from other religions and hence they may be reluctant to accept this insight as part of their understanding. The traditional Trinity of 'Father, Son and Holy Spirit' has served the Church well. In particular, it expresses the relationship between the First and Second Persons far better than does the present model, even though this can then imply a lesser relationship between either of the first two persons and the third.

There may be value in tempering the old with the new, so that we obtain a Gardening-Father, a Loving-Son and a Dancing-Spirit. This retains the tradition whilst adding new insights which may provoke further thought. The adjectives for the Son and the Holy Spirit should not cause any problem; Jesus is clearly a loving-son. However, the gardening nature of the Father may be more of a cause for discussion. It may serve to down-play the absolute patriarchal nature with which the Father is often credited and which has the fault that it overshadows the insights of the Son and Spirit. It may also remind us that God has a concern for the whole of His creation, and that the environmental crisis which has been taken as the present theological context is unlikely to qualify for the divine description of 'Good'.

The gardening metaphor for God The Father can also serve to remind us of another important aspect of Creation, namely that of 'play'. The Gardening God is the God who takes play seriously and who puts it to purposeful creative effect. This is the God who knows about hard work which brings with it the satisfaction of a job well done when He sees that it is 'good'. This is the God who can sit back at the end of the hard 'day' and relax as He views His handiwork. This is the God who knows that things are important in their own right and not because of what they can do for Him. This is the God who wants His followers – The Church – to discover the same things for themselves.

Notes

1. See, for instance, Wren pp.3ff and McFague pp.3ff.
2. Peacocke (1979) pp.38ff; See also Nicholls p.241.
3. Wren p.61 (see also p.3).
4. Ramsey (1971).
5. E.g. Soskice (1985).

6. See Ramsey (1971), p.208.

7. This definition is taken from p.15 of Soskice (1985), see also pp.43ff. and Wren pp.84ff.

8. Tillich (1978a) pp.235ff, see also (1978b) p.9.

9. See Donovan, pp.95ff.

10. Soskice (1985), pp.97ff; Ramsey (1971).

11. Barbour pp.41–51.

12. An example might be the atomic model in which particulate electrons are pictured as orbiting about a central nucleus. In this model the mathematics is actually subservient to the 'picture', for it was the picture which came first and the mathematics was then used to describe the scene.

13. Barbour pp.41ff.

14. Ramsey (1971) pp.213f.

15. Ramsey (1971) pp.211ff.

16. The implications of this for theology in the modern world have been explored by Polkinghorne (1983) in his book of the same title.

17. Moltmann (1985) p.297.

18. McFague p.33.

19. Song pp.45ff.

20. McFague pp.xif, 18f.

21. This difference is discussed in chapter one of Dillistone.

22. Gregory Nazianzus, 'Fourth Theological Oration', i.e. *30*.17, as quoted by Jantzen (1984) p.1. Note that Jantzen erroneously refers to this as the Second Theological Oration.

23. McFague pp.22f, pp.35ff.

24. This argument recurs throughout Wren, see especially pp.4 and 52.

25. See Moltmann (1981) pp.34–36, where he comments on Studdert Kennedy's work 'The Hardest Part'.

26. Pannenberg (1991) pp.259ff.

27. Pannenberg (1991) p.262.

28. McFague pp.64–68.

29. Stephen Sykes has made a similar criticism of McFague's insistence on the aggressive nature of the 'hierarchical, imperialistic, patriarchal model'. He sees her views as being a product of the American approach to exploitative power; see p.x of his introduction to Hodgson and King.

30. See, for instance, Calvert pp.18f.

31. Nicholls p.243.

32. McFague pp.45ff.

33. Wren Ch.5.

34. Wren pp.208ff.

35. Epistle 38.8, sometimes attributed to Gregory of Nyssa and quoted here from page 264 of Kelly.

36. Quoted by Wren pp.155ff.

37. McFague pp.78ff and throughout.

38. McFague pp.98ff.

39. Wren pp.155ff.

40. Wren p.209.

41. Wren p.210.

42. For example, Genesis Ch.1 v2 has the *ruach*, the Spirit (or Wind) of God, moving over the waters. The Pentecost experience in Acts Ch.2 v1ff is accompanied by a mighty wind and tongues of fire. Water has come to be associated with the grace of God received through the Holy Spirit at baptism, although the words of John the Baptist do distinguish between baptism by water and baptism in the Holy Spirit. The Holy Spirit also appeared as a dove at the baptism of Jesus, e.g. Matthew Ch.3 v16.

43. Macquarrie (1975) p.129.

44. For further details see, for instance, Moltmann (1985) p.298, 301.

45. For example, see Hendry pp.154ff.

46. Vanstone (1977) pp.30ff.

47. This simile is present in Jeremiah Ch.18 v4ff.

48. Peacocke (1979) p.105.

49. Daly (1988) pp.34ff, 40f.

50. Notable examples occur in Psalm 23, Ezekiel Ch.34 and John Ch.10.

51. McFague p.13; Wren pp.237ff.

52. The idea of a garden is found, for example, in Genesis Ch.2 v8 and Isaiah Ch.58 v11, whilst that of a vineyard is found in Isaiah Ch.5 vv1–7 amongst other places.

53. Matthew Ch.20 vv1–16, Ch.21 vv33–41 and parallels.

54. The New English Bible and The New International Version both use the translation 'gardener', whilst the Revised Standard Version uses 'vine-dresser'.

55. Bultmann p.531.

56. Vanstone (1977) pp.39ff, 57ff.

57. Wisdom pp.149–168.

58. Macquarrie (1975) pp.114–116.

59. Tillich (1978c) pp.145–146.

60. Williams pp.15–16 and p.21.

61. Williams pp.19–20.

62. McFadyen (1992) pp.14–15.

63. Pannenberg (1991) p.329; Moltmann (1974) pp.241ff.

64. Moltmann (1985) pp.304–307.

65. See Moltmann (1985) p.305 and Peacocke (1979) p.107.

Chapter 7

A Playful Christian Response

In the preceding chapters we have examined the ways in which Christian doctrine is able to respond to the challenge of an increasing concern for the environment. However, Christianity is not merely a system of ideas and beliefs, but is rather a whole way of life which includes tradition, experience and ritual as well as theological arguments. In order to move the debate on further, there is therefore a need to address the question as to how the life of the Church, through its organisation and its worship, can be relevant to the present situation. In answering this question, the response should not be focused on specific environmental programmes, as the methods and details of such activities are already available from secular agencies. It should instead concentrate on providing a distinctly Christian approach which can exist alongside and complement such environmental programmes. The present discussion will therefore focus on the ways in which care for the whole creation can be part of the living Christian tradition of ecclesiology and worship without this care being an extra imposed from the outside.

7.1 Three Modern Heresies

Members of the Christian Church are called upon to be holy: a part of the world in which they live, and yet also set apart from and against that world. This same call applies to the Church itself, in that it exists within the world and yet it should also point beyond the purely material towards that which is divine. In this respect it is instructive to consider which aspects of the present world are contrary to Christian teaching and which the Church should therefore reject or attempt to change. In particular, it is important to consider how the Church can ensure that those aspects of society which lie at the roots of the environmental crisis are absent from its own life. It is only after this has been done that the Church will be fit to put into practice a distinctly Christian approach to the problem.

In making this consideration, it is useful to remind ourselves of the distinction between Sin and sins (see section 2.3). This distinction implies that rather than examining particular examples of behaviour which are felt to be undesirable, such as air pollution from power stations, we should instead consider the underlying beliefs which manifest themselves in these particular actions. When considering environmental problems, these underlying beliefs are principally those of western civilization.

The principles which underlie western society are increasingly being adopted throughout the world, as a result of a widely held belief that these are fundamental to the attainment of a higher standard of living.[1] The present premise is that it is this set of principles which lie at the root of the environmental crisis and that as they spread, so the problem will become worse. The question to be addressed is not that of how we can replace a particular lifestyle and what we should replace it with, rather it is to identify the particular assumptions within society which cause the problems. Once identified, these assumptions can be seen both as ideas which the Church should reject, as well as issues which the wider society should address.

There are three characteristics of the western lifestyle which can be shown to be contrary to the teaching of Christian theology. This criticism is not affected by the support which Christian Puritanism and the Protestant work-ethic have given to these tenets in portraying them as part of a higher morality. They occur throughout contemporary culture, whether it be work, music, politics, social structures or the whole style of the modern economic enterprise. These characteristics are busyness, usefulness and an unrelenting belief in success. In the effect which they can have on Christian belief and practice, it is probably accurate to describe them as three modern heresies.

7.1.1 Busyness

Busyness is often portrayed as a virtue in itself and can develop into an insidious feeling that if we are not doing something then we are in the wrong. This idea has found its way into folk-lore with sayings such as 'The devil makes work for idle hands', a saying which is sometimes used to criticise people who have the time to play rather than being busy. Yet there is evidence in both scripture and tradition that this point of view is in error. In the account of Jesus' visit to the home of Martha and Mary given in Luke Ch.10 vv38-42, Martha is deliberately rebuked for her busyness, whilst Mary is commended for simply sitting with Jesus. Mary is told that she has chosen the better part. There is the ever-present risk, both within the Church and in society, that if we concentrate too much on 'doing' then we shall lose touch with our spiritual roots. This state of affairs is parallelled in secular society where many people work increasingly long hours. When Christianity is associated with this work-ethic, it is unable to meet the needs of those who reject this situation and who are seeking out a new spiritual dimension in their lives. Christian teaching can come to be seen as incompatible with the idea of a relaxed and meditative lifestyle which would be more in tune with the pace of the natural world.

The most fundamental objection to busyness within the Judaeo-Christian tradition is provided by the Sabbath – the tradition of rest on the seventh day of the week – a tradition which has come to be misunderstood and misused. In the Jewish Law, the Sabbath was not simply a weekly day-off for members of the human race; it was a day of rest for everything – creatures as well as humanity. Nor was the Sabbath confined to one day each week. It also encompassed Sabbath years during which land was allowed to lie fallow, and the year of Jubilee when everything that was in slavery was allowed to go free. This principle, codified in Laws so that it might be enforced, was in effect a statement that everything within the creation needs a time of rest and relaxation.

In the creation narratives, we find a more fundamental state-ment about rest, in God's decision to rest on the seventh day of creation after He had finished His work (Genesis Ch.2 vv1-4a). As Gerhard von Rad noted, this account is not concerned with the institution of the Sabbath, but is about God sanctifying the rest which the world is to share with Him.[2] It is a statement of God's completion of His work of creation, a work which he completed on the seventh day and not on the sixth as is often thought to be the case. The work of creation was completed with the creation of rest and the Sabbath Day is the feast or festival of the Sabbath as discussed in much more detail by Moltmann.[3] As Jesus Himself noted, echoing thoughts which were present in parts of the Jewish tradition, 'The Sabbath was made for man, not man for the Sabbath' (Mark, Ch.2 v27). The Sabbath is God's gift of rest and recuperation.

In the Church itself, we can learn a great deal from the divine blessing upon rest, coupled with the lesson from Martha and Mary. Our lives are so often occupied with the busyness of committees, administration and fund-raising that we can easily lose sight of the real meaning and purpose which lies behind all that we do. We need to find time for God as Godself, rather than a continual busyness which is focused on the outward trappings of religion and its organisation rather than being based upon God. In short, the heresy that it is good to be busy can prevent us from simply being still and waiting upon God. It can also blind us to the possibility that such waiting can actually be part of what it is to be made in the image of God. This idea of waiting and its vital role in the Passion of Christ have been discussed in detail by Bill Vanstone.[4] An unrelenting busyness can also lead us to adopt quick and easy answers to problems whereas a longer-term approach could be more friendly to the environment. In order to be Holy, the Church has to separate itself from the continual busyness which exists within the world.

7.1.2 Usefulness

The second modern heresy is that of usefulness. Here there are two distinct strands of thought. The first is that everything, whether plant, animal or object, must have a purpose. The second is that everything which we do must be useful.

The problem with everything needing to have a purpose, is that this purpose is, in general, defined from a human perspective in terms of whether things are useful to us. The Christian belief in a creative God should not allow us to take such an anthropocentric view. The divine statement that creation is good should override any notion of usefulness. This is supported by the belief that we are loved by God and that the Son of God died for us on the cross not because of anything which we had done but as a free gift of His grace. In short, God does not love us because we are useful, but loves us as a free and undeserved gift. If we are made in the image of God and are the stewards of His creation, then our stewardship should be characterised by a similar gift of grace and not by whether things are useful.

Turning to the second of the above ideas, namely that all we do should be useful, we first remark that to base our lives on the idea of being useful is to remove a dimension from our existence. If we always want to be active in this way then we cut ourselves off from the possibility of genuine play and from its potential for creativity. We can concentrate so much on doing things which appear to be useful, that we can forget how to play and in the process lose our ability to be creative.

The psychologist Eric Rayner has described play as being an active but relaxed manipulation of materials, with the note that these materials may be either physical or mental.[5] In the case of children these materials are usually physical, although we should note the significance which can be placed on these materials by the mental processes of the child. In everyday adult conversation, the play of children is usually treated as a low-level activity, something which is of secondary importance to work. This description misses the true importance of play and ignores the fact that for those who are truly involved within it, play is a very serious business.

The adult description of play as a second rate activity (children know better), is related both to our idea of work and to the emergence of a leisure industry and culture. For the adult, the major emphasis in life is usually on labour or work rather than on play, and play can then become merely an escape from work.[6] Although playing is preferable to working, work is seen as more useful, with the result that any genuine involvement in play for its own sake can produce a feeling of guilt.

In the years preceding his consecration as Bishop of Durham, David Jenkins noted that many people now live in what can be termed a leisure culture. In such a culture many people discover that work occupies less of their time than in earlier generations and that there is a need to search for alternative activities. This results in the opportunity to rediscover play.[7] However, much of this play is contrived and non-genuine and the participants are still deprived of genuine play. Jenkins seems to agree with this comment, for he notes that the play of a leisure-culture is bourgeois and involves an avoidance of responsibility,[8] whereas we shall discover that genuine play is not guilty of this charge.

In addition to dispelling the myth that play is a second-rate activity, we must also avoid the idea that all play is the same. It has long been realized that there are a number of different types of play in which we can be involved. These include: free-play which exists for its own sake and has no prescribed boundaries; creative-play which exists for a defined purpose; drama, which follows a set plan, but which involves the participants in creativity and imagination; organised-play, which follows a set of rules; and constructional-play, which allows free movement toward a goal.[9] Part of the difficulty with analyzing the play of adults, is that it is often difficult to define what counts as play. In his writings on the growth of human personality, J.H. Kahn has noted that what is play for one person can be the business or profession of another.[10] Most sports and artistic fields illustrate this point.

At first sight, the linking of theology and play can appear to be a contradiction of terms. It can be argued that theology is a serious business whereas play is much lighter. However, if we examine play in detail, we discover that this objection is not valid. Theology is a serious business, but play is also serious and is deeply concerned with reality. The North-American theologian Harvey Cox, who uses the word 'festivity' in a way which is very similar to the psychologists' use of 'play', notes that not only is festivity not superficial, but that it also recognises tragedy and enables its participants to cope with this tragedy.[11]

The recognition of play as a serious business and its ability to cope with tragedy allows us to make the connection with theology. At the very least we should recognise that Christian theology has to make sense of the life of Jesus of Nazareth, a life which in the classical dramatic sense would be described as a tragedy which is then transformed into a comedy through the postscript of the resurrection. Theology also has to deal with tragedy in the issues of theodicy, evil and what we can describe as fallen human nature. If play is the way in which human-beings come to terms with the problems which face us in the world, and this is certainly the case with much of children's play, then play and theology are more closely related than appears to be the case at first sight.

This approach is similar to that taken by Moltmann when he asks the question with which the negro slaves echoed the Babylonian exiles; 'How can I play in a strange land?' How, he asks, can we play when we have so many cares and worries about us, when children starve and terrorists plant bombs and kill people?[12] Moltmann makes the point that play is for those who mourn, that it is a means of dealing with the real problems of life. True play is a liberating experience and not the indulgent play of good fortune which is cut off from what is real.[13]

The modern heresy of usefulness also affects the way in which we perceive God. The knowledge that true fulfilment is impossible in ourselves and only achievable through the grace of God produces a tendency in which God is regarded as useful and is discussed in terms of what He can do for us. Jenkins describes this process as making God tidy and controlled rather than making an expansive commitment to Him.[14] We want to understand all about God so as to make best use of Him, and we take exception to those people who disagree us.

A god who is merely useful is an idol, a creation of the human mind. True God is worshipped for His own self irrespective of any utility value which He may possess. The traditional (and false) picture of man as a doer of duty under a dominating god has caused political, ecclesiastical and psychological problems and has been seen as part of the cause of the ecological crisis. It is also a barrier to faith. People either reject what they see as a false God or else turn away from a God who is worshipped by others for His utility but is of no relevance to them. We can sympathize with Nietzsche's 'Death of God' and with Freud's rejection of the God whom he saw as a transition object, in as much as the god whom Freud and Nietzsche rejected is in fact the god of a distorted and demeaning human projection and not the true God whom we are called to worship freely.[15]

7.1.3 Success

The third modern heresy is that of the unrelenting belief in success. We live in a world in which success is even more important than busyness or usefulness. Success is the criterion against which everything often appears to be judged. In many professions, the success of individuals is now measured by means of pre-determined criteria known as 'performance indicators' and in sport the joy and purpose of participation and simply playing the game are increasingly sacrificed to the necessity of winning and the possibility of financial reward. Although performance against set standards (whether in exams or in personal appraisal) can be a good thing, it becomes dangerous if it is taken to excess and made the principal criterion in judging a person's life.

We find the same standards within the Church. The success of a particular local Church is increasingly judged by the number of people in the congregation and whether the size of this congregation is increasing or decreasing.[16] Similarly, statistics are kept on the numbers of baptisms and marriages conducted in Church and these are again used as criteria of success or failure. Individual Christians are often challenged as to whether they are spiritually 'good enough', or whether they are good enough Christians at all. This challenge is often made in comparison to a particular style of churchmanship or spirituality which might be quite alien to the person concerned.

These approaches to success are misleading. For an individual, salvation is not determined by how good we are as Christians (although that is no excuse not to try) but by the grace of God. In the case of the wider principle, the use of success as a guide-line imposes the standards of the world onto the God who has different criteria. By worldly standards, Jesus of Nazareth was a complete failure. He ended His life by being executed on a cross with His disciples deserting and disowning Him. The Christian belief is that this apparent failure was an essential part of a resounding success. It was fundamental in the defeat of the forces of evil and in the divine triumph over Sin.

7.2 The Need to Play

In all three of these modern heresies there is a contrast between the wisdom of the world and the wisdom of God. The question as to whether the death of Jesus of Nazareth on the cross was a failure or a success provides a summary of this difference. As St. Paul wrote to the Church at Corinth:

> 'Where is the wise man? Where is the scribe? Where is the debater of this age? Has not God made foolish the wisdom of the world? For since, in the wisdom of God, the world did not know God through wisdom, it pleased God through the folly of what we preach to save those who believe. For Jews demand signs and Greeks seek wisdom, but we preach Christ crucified, a stumbling-block to Jews and folly to Gentiles, but to those who are called, both Jews and Greeks, Christ the power of God and the wisdom of God. For the foolishness of God is wiser than men, and the weakness of God is stronger than men. (I Cor. Ch.*1*. vv20-25, RSV)

At the heart of the Christian life there is a tension between involvement with God and involvement with the world. The Christian faith exists within this tension. The more agonizing or glorious the world and the life which we lead within the world, then the more we need the mystery of God to provide us with a different perspective. Within the Church, we need continually to remind ourselves of the foolishness of God and of the fact that God's ways are not the same as the ways of the world. We need to relearn the lesson that we should not always trust to the wisdom of the passing age. We need to rediscover the significance of God's ways and the central tenets of the Christian faith, together with the way in which these can become an integral part of our lives rather than an add-on extra.

In 1948, Paul Tillich wrote a book entitled 'The Protestant Era'. Part of this work was concerned with the decline in Protestantism during a period of time which Tillich described as the 'Post-Protestant Era'. He saw this era as characterised by the loss of the central doctrine of justification by grace through faith.[17] Tillich believed that this loss had occurred because of a decline in the intelligibility of the doctrine in a culture where man strives towards his own autonomy and in which he believes that he is self-reliant and master of all. This is a culture in which the concepts of justification and salvation are irrelevant because they do not depend on our own efforts. It could be said that religion had become an overly serious business and had lost the joy and spontaneity which results from the knowledge of God's love and what He has done for us.

Tillich saw the need for humanity to realise the presence of an unconditional threat to its collective and individual existence so that it could rediscover God's free gift of grace and respond accordingly. He believed that it knew this threat intellectually, but no longer possessed as part of its fundamental and deep-seated beliefs about life. Tillich rejected human attempts to escape from the threat to our existence and pointed to the need for us to believe that we are accepted by that which is beyond us; that salvation rests with God and not with ourselves. Salvation is a gift of grace and cannot be achieved by intellectual theories or truths any more than it can be by attempts at moral goodness.[18]

Tillich blamed Protestantism itself for the above decline and its own downfall. He believed that this had occurred because of its persistent stress on individual salvation at the expense of collective responsibility. A religion, ethic or philosophy which stresses individualism at the expense of the wider community, runs the risk of finally persuading an individual that he does not need the religion, ethic or philosophy either, because it too comes from beyond himself. Whether or not Tillich was correct about Protestantism, his critical description certainly applies to the underlying principles of the present age.

Tillich saw religion becoming increasingly wordy and bound by regulations. He protested that the Christian faith is not about a theoretical affirmation, but is a state of being grasped by God. He saw a devaluing of the value, worth and place of sacraments, symbols and mysticism, with authority being vested in the words of theology alone. Religion was being increasingly circumscribed by rationality and exchanging its power of celebration for a tedious monotony.[19] For Tillich there were three pointers to the way forward for the Church in his day, three ways in which it could rediscover its vitality whilst being relevant to the modern age. Whatever their validity at that time, these pointers describe the way in which the Church can respond to the needs of the world at the present time and in particular the way in which it can respond to the environmental crisis.

First, the Church should maintain a prophetic voice and protest against anything in the world which claims to have absolute power or knowledge. It should do this not as an apologetic or proof of the existence of God, but as a reminder of the transitory nature of human life and of our achievements. We are finite beings and cannot grasp the whole of the situation in which we exist. This prophetic voice should be exercised in the full knowledge of human Sin and the misuse of human power. In the present day such human knowledge and power is not a good reason for environmental exploitation. The prophetic voice of the Christian Church needs to speak out against such actions on the grounds of the human place within the wider purposes of God and our lack of such knowledge, in addition to the usual argument that God described His creation as 'Good'.

Secondly, the Church needs to rediscover its symbols and sacraments and redevelop its interest in mysticism. Human words are insufficient to reach to the hearts of people. A religion without meaningful symbols and sacraments which point to the divine is no longer a religion. The new nature religions and pagan cults make extensive use of natural symbolism and the mysticism of the natural world. If Christianity becomes devoid of meaningful symbols which relate to the world in which it exists or if it uses them in a slipshod manner devoid of quality or relevance, then we should not be surprised if Christianity cannot meet the spiritual needs of the world. This point is particularly relevant to many of the prayers and liturgies which have been introduced during the second half of the twentieth century. They offer the advantages of being understandable, relevant, theologically 'correct' and are better suited to the present day than are their precursors in almost every respect. Their one fault is that, in general, their words are not evocative. They speak too much to the intellect and not enough to the heart. They fail to create pictures within us because they have lost their sense of poetry. They fail to evoke the joy we should feel at being alive as a part of God's creation.

Thirdly, as we noted in chapter two, there is the issue of 'Belief-ful Realism', which Tillich believed should describe our relationship with the world. Realism, in the sense that Christianity is concerned with the real world as it exists, and belief-ful in the sense that we acknowledge its relationship with God and that God can be known through the natural world. This is an approach which allows God to be at the centre of all life. It is not a form of pantheism, for it is not belief in the world, but it is rather an approach which acknowledges the relationship of that world with God. It breaks down the tension which can exist when Christianity has to hold together its involvement with the world and its involvement with God. This belief-ful approach is not confined to the natural world, but also extends to art and other products of human creativity. It serves to remind us that Christ is the saviour of the whole World and not only of the Church.

Belief-ful Realism is close to being a human expression of perichoresis, which can be described as an approach in which we make room for the world about us, rather than environing the World and hemming it in. If perichoresis is the best way in which we can talk about the Divine Trinity then it should also be able to express our relationships within the world. In talking about God, the perichoretic activity of the Trinity is described in terms of its mutual-communion or κοινωνια.[20] If the Church is true to these principles then it should mark them through its own κοινωνια or community and through the way in which this κοινωνια extends to the whole of God's Creation.

These arguments suggest that we are called on to respond to God in a way which is marked by a radical openness both to God and to His creation; the kind of response and openness which we make to someone when we are in love with them or when we engage in genuine play with them. However, human relationships are affected by our fallen nature and this radical openness can only be achieved through the indwelling presence of the Holy Spirit and the presence of the Word of God about us. In short, it can only be achieved by grace. McFadyen has described this as Christ the Word bringing redemption and order to our structures and relationships, thereby allowing true personhood.[21] At the same time the Holy Spirit brings life to our structures and thereby makes them dynamic and sustains them in a state of openness to the world.

In our working to save the creation we should remember that we are ourselves saved by grace. This implies that we should not be unduly legalistic in our approach to environmental problems. Wherever possible we should work by consent rather than coercion. It also implies that if we are to act according to the divine image in which we are made, then we should ensure the survival of species and environments which cannot justify themselves to us by their usefulness, beauty or any other criteria which we devise. We should do this because we cannot justify ourselves before God but have instead to rely upon His grace. We need to relearn how to play in a free and spontaneous manner in the world which God has made. The whole approach of the Church to the Divine Creation should be typified by this attitude of genuine play.

7.3 The Nature of Play

What does it mean to play? In order to answer this question we first need to find a summary of what constitutes play and the motivating factors which lead people to engage in this activity. Such a summary can usefully be provided as a list of the principal characteristics of play, together with a summary of the rules which have developed to govern its conduct and a list of the factors which motivate true play. No two authors agree on the precise contents of these lists and those given here have been compiled from the works of Winicott[22] and Kahn[23] who have both written extensively on this subject. We shall first consider the characteristics of play, then examine the ways in which rules can emerge and develop with time and finally attempt to list some of the principal factors which can motivate the play which is described by these characteristics and rules.

The characteristics of play

(i)   One of the most important characteristics of play is that things become other than themselves; that they take on a symbolic value to the players which can seem quite absurd to an outside observer. An important development of this point is the observation that although all symbols contain a degree of ambiguity, an obsessional child or adult will want to know the one true meaning of a particular symbol and will only tolerate that one meaning, taking care to deny all others and to avoid them.[24]

(ii)   A second important characteristic of play is that much of the activity has the purpose of preparing its participants for the future. It helps them to cope with events· with which they will be involved but which they have not yet experienced. A simple example is that young children often play at being parents.

(iii) A third characteristic, which follows on from the second and applies especially to children, is that the participants often play at being bigger and stronger, such as teachers or doctors. In this way, they anticipate the day when they can overcome the problems which they encounter or perceive within the world.

(iv)   A fourth characteristic is that when play is interrupted or the rules are suddenly changed from the outside, then this can cause distress to those participants who have not yet finished with that particular form of play. This is especially the case if the participants were poorly adapted to whatever they were resolving through that play. This disruption can then lead to compulsive play of the requisite type.

(v)   Fifthly, play is spontaneous and undertaken by free will. Children who are told to go and play will often resent the fact. True play cannot occur by coercion.

(vi) Sixthly, play is enjoyable and is often engaged in for its own sake with no other purpose. Play does not have to be useful in a worldly sense.

(vii) Finally, play is real. It is not a second rate activity designed to fill a space in our lives, but a serious business of real importance to those who are involved in it. This is still the case even when it appears to be nonsense to the outside observer. An example would be an adult who spends his 'spare-time' building model railways.

If we now consider the rules of play, we discover that although these vary a great deal, they tend to follow certain common patterns.

The rules which govern play

(i)   We first note that rules tend to emerge rather than being imposed, although it is sometimes possible for an accepted authority figure to introduce a modification to the existing set of rules. In general, there is a mutual agreement among the participants as to the content of the rules and those players who continue to disagree will eventually leave. The nineteenth century division of football into soccer and rugby demonstrated this point.

(ii) Secondly, the rules of play are often highly complex, and as much time can be spent in producing and debating the rules as is devoted to the actual play itself. This applies just as much to the genuine play of small children as it does to the contrived play of organised sports.

(iii) Thirdly, the presence of established rules frees participants from the worry about the practical details of their activity, because these details have already been dealt with.

(iv) Fourthly, rules are never inviolate. They are inevitably broken at various times by most of the players. This occurs not only through accidents but also in order to investigate the consequences of such behaviour. Such challenges to the authority of the regulations can eventually result in an accepted change.

(v)   A fifth point about rules takes the form of an internal rule which emerges as play changes with time. This is that too much novelty is confusing to the participants but that too little novelty results in sensory deprivation and boredom. This should be remembered by those adults who supervise children at play and who want to guide them in a sensible direction. A child will often ignore new toys and return to an old favourite but the old favourite alone will result in boredom.

The factors which motivate play

In his normative article 'Why Children Play', Donald Winnicott summarized five motivating factors for children at play.[25] These reasons can easily be extended to people of all ages.

(i)   It is important to recognise that the first reason for play is that of pleasure. In our analysis of their hidden motives it is easy for us to lose sight of the fact that children play because they enjoy it. A child who is genuinely engrossed in play is a happy child. If we stop enjoying an activity then it can no longer be described as genuine play.

(ii)   A second reason for play is to express aggression. This is partly to work off the aggression, but also to experiment with the way in which aggression works and the effects of aggression whilst remaining within a controlled environment.

(iii) Similar motives lie behind the third reason for play, namely that play is motivated by gaining experience; the idea of learning by doing. Children have always played in order to learn by doing, despite its supposed discovery by educationalists in the late nineteen-fifties and early nineteen-sixties. Kahn describes this as recapitulation, an activity in which children resolve the experiences of the past day by reliving them in their play.

(iv) This then leads onto the fourth reason for play, namely
      that of making social contacts and of communication with
      people. This involves experimentation in how we express
      our inner self and how our inner self can relate to the
      world around us. We can observe this in the behaviour of
      a child when an adult does not understand what it is
      telling them or what it is trying to ask. The child is often
      incredulous at the adult's lack of understanding because it
      knows what it is trying to say. Its problem is that it has
      not yet learnt the full range of expressions which are
      needed in order to communicate the idea successfully.
(v)   Winnicott finally notes that play enables a child to master
      anxiety via experimentation with surrogates and helps it
      to integrate its personality.

It is interesting that Winnicott's listing appears to concentrate
exclusively on the past except where it involves imitating
adults so as to prepare to fulfil the same roles in the future. It
is possible that this concentration is due to his Freudian background. Kahn adds an additional motivating factor for play,
namely that of anticipation, in which the child prepares to cope
with the future where that future is largely unknown. This has
important implications for the examination of play in the life of
the Church as we shall see below. For the moment we shall
simply note that different people are able to cope with change
and the unexpected much more easily than others and that this
ability may be partly related to the way in this has been anticipated in play at an earlier age.

7.4 The Church at Play

Before we can answer the question of how the rules and characteristics of play apply to the Church, we need to consider
exactly what we mean by the word 'Church' and how a Church
might operate. Although there are clearly many definitions of
what constitutes the Church, one possible definition is that
provided by the Hanson brothers, who stated that, 'The
Church is the People of God and it is called to be the Body of
Christ.'[26] If we turn our attention to the way in which the

Church operates, we should note the work of Avery Dulles as expressed in his book 'Models of the Church'.[27] If we take each of Dulles' five models in turn, we can ask the question of how the Church, as portrayed in that model, can be understood in terms of the characteristics, rules and reasons for play which we examined in section 7.3.

Taking first the model of The Church as Institution, Dulles defines this as a visible society which is ruled and organized by a structural government which is itself hierarchical, judgemental and triumphalistic. Although such a church has a corporate identity and a continuity with the past, the laity are passive and there is a high role for human authority. The traditional understanding of the Roman Catholic Church provides an example which is close to this description. Within such a Church, play can be described as 'play for the masses', in which there is a parent-child relationship between the clergy and the people. This is similar to the idea which we noted above in which adults often regard play as something which is for children; something which keeps them happy and occupied. This similarity is emphasised by the fact that in this model, the form and rules of the play are imposed from above. The game is largely beyond the control of the participants. This is the reason why additional popular accretions of myth and piety often occur within churches which approximate to this model. They are rules which have been added by the players. If we had to use the categories of Winnicott to select reasons for being involved in play of this type, then we might want to choose those of mastering anxiety and making social contact.

Dulles' second model is that of The Church as Mystical Communion. This is characterized by an informal community which regards itself as indwelt by the Holy Spirit. Personal relationships are fostered and relational needs are met. According to Dulles, the problems which can occur within such a church are those of exclusivism and the fact that the Church can become so wrapped up within itself that it misses the importance of mission to those who are on the outside. In terms of play, it is quite likely that this environment will foster the emergence of true play, provided that these distortions do not occur, although it can also lead to the assumption that no play is possible elsewhere. If we are interested in authentic play then this model has much to commend it. The problems which can occur within such play are the possibility of the emergence of a rigid set of rules, as in forms of pietism, and that the players can become so engrossed in their play that they lose contact with the outside world. Dulles questions why anybody would want to join such a church. If genuine play is present within this Church and Dulles is standing outside the model, then his question is understandable but misses the point that we can only understand this Church from the inside. It is the same question as that asked by the adult who cannot understand the very real and engrossing play of children.

Moving on to the third model, we find The Church as Sacrament. Here, the divine and human are inseparable. Structures are not enough because the Church is only the Church through the grace of God. The Church calls for loyalty from its members but, as a sacrament, it points beyond itself to God. Dulles' criticism of this model is that it can lead to the lack of an inner spiritual life, because it is so concerned with what is beyond the self. In terms of play, it is as if the whole of the play were to become a single symbol rather than play being symbolic and containing many symbols within itself. Within the model there is an abundance of material with which to play (the whole of God and His creation) and this may be so overwhelming that genuine play can be lacking. To the new initiate in such a church there may be the classic problem of just too much input to assimilate and an overloading of the senses. In addition, the external constraints placed on the participants may be so powerful that the emergence of true play is stifled.

The Church as Herald is a kerygmatic model, centred on the cross and involved in outreach to the world. The Church is seen as authentically present in each local assembly via the presence of the Word of God. There is no dependence on outside structures and there is a strong sense of mission and evangelism – the process of taking the good news to those who have not yet heard it. This model is typified by an independent Evangelical Church or an Evangelical Church which regards its links to other Churches within its Communion as less important than its own understanding of the Word of God.

Dulles' criticism of this model is that it denies the Universal Church and that it is focused entirely on witness, with no social policy or action. As a result, when we try to relate this model to play we encounter a problem. It is as if the players are spending so much time trying to persuade others to join their game that they have no time to play it themselves. There also appears to be some sort of assumption that other groups of players (the members of other local churches) should be playing in the same way and using the same rules. If they are not playing in this same way, then they should change. In this model, the self-confident approach of the players means that they never need to play for any of the reasons which Winnicott suggests. Either genuine play has been left behind and is no longer needed, or else the members are missing out on an important aspect of their lives.

Dulles' model is of course a caricature, an extreme example given precisely to make the point. However, it is recognisable in certain confident 'evangelical' churches who, whilst proclaiming their redeemed status, fail to recognise their present sin which manifests itself in internal disputes of various kinds. This suggests that play has not been outgrown but is instead seriously lacking and has a vital role to play in the life of such a Church. Churches which do fit the 'Herald' model need to relearn how to play, and to adopt practices from other models of the Church.

Finally, we turn to the model of The Church as Servant. This is a model which takes the world seriously. It follows the line of Bonhoeffer that the Church is only the Church as it exists for others. The Church has to be relevant to the world through its service in the world. Dulles asks the question as to how such a Church can relate to the Kingdom of God. This Church might answer that its role is to transform the world into the Kingdom. Such a Church runs the risk of losing sight of God in its attempt to be relevant to the world and thereby becoming little more than a social welfare organisation. From the perspective of play, we might ask how it is possible for us to play in the Kingdom if we are always serving others. We run the risk of merely being useful and failing to exist for our own sake, failing to play for its own sake and failing to worship God for God's own sake. Our play becomes professional and institutionalized, or at best a leisure industry of service to others. We may move towards mastering anxiety, express our aggression and make social contacts, we may even think that we gain pleasure, but our play is deficient. Taken in isolation the servant model is inadequate. Play is not merely useful. In this respect we should note the thoughts of Kierkegaard, who wrote that in seeking the Kingdom of God, the action which is required is not to indulge in any particular action in terms of worldly activity, but to keep silent and to seek the Kingdom of God.[28] We seek the Kingdom of God by seeking the Kingdom of God and not by doing something else.

None of these five models should be expected to work in isolation, although many churches do approximate closely to one model or another. What should be clear from this discussion, is that both the Church at large and local churches can engage in play in ways which are identical to those of other groups of people. This should not be a surprise, but it is worth noting and we might want to ask what our own model or models can teach us about our local church community. The key question which we need to answer is whether the Church possesses a particular style of play in which it alone can engage. If it does have such a style of play, what can our analysis of play tell us about this activity and about the way in which it enables the Church to relate to God and to care for and play in His Creation?

Hugo Rahner has described play as follows:

'To play is to yield oneself to a kind of magic, to enact to oneself the absolutely other, to pre-empt the future, to give the lie to the inconvenient world of fact. In play, earthly realities become, of a sudden, things of the transient moment, presently left behind, then disposed of and buried in the past; the mind is prepared to accept the unimagined and incredible, to enter a world where different laws apply, to be relieved of all the weights that bear it down, to be free, kingly, unfettered and divine.[29]

Harvey Cox has remarked that this description could almost be a description of prayer,[30] presumably prayer in its broadest sense, including both meditation and contemplation. Cox notes that the prayer of supplication is to place ourselves in the nonexistent future and that intercessory prayer allows us to identify with another person's situation and to look into their future. In both of these cases there is a parallel with the way in which play can also help us to cope with the unknown contents of the future.

Both play and prayer move beyond the immediate world of fact and transcend it in a different state of reality. Of course this does not apply to prayer by rote, nor to the situation where prayers are said because we are told to do so. In this context, prayer refers to a much deeper experience in which there is either true communion with God or a true and anguished longing for communion with God. This distinction between prayer and forced prayer offers a direct parallel with the difference between true play and the play of children who have been told to go out and play.

Prayer is not the only way in which we can find distinctive play in the Church; indeed, prayer by itself is probably too individualistic to reflect the play of a corporate body. The Mirfield Father and liturgist George Guiver has noted that, like play, prayer has an uncertain outcome which is unpredictable in advance. He then goes on to draw the same conclusion about worship.[31] It has been noted that to the outsider worship can look just like play in that it appears to serve no worldly purpose. The present contention is that although the church does play in ways which are exactly the same as those of other groups of people, its unique method of play occurs in prayer and especially in its worship. Oppenheimer has described worship as a free response to God in our relationship with Him.[32] Such a free response in worship is similar to the freedom of spontaneous action which occurs in play. The consequences of this relationship between play and worship are discussed below in chapter eight.

If it is important for the church to be able to play, then it is pertinent to ask what factors might prevent it from doing so. In his introduction to Moltmann's 'Theology of Joy', David Jenkins noted the work of Paul Verghese, who identified five distortions in theology which he believed originated in the teaching of Augustine of Hippo.[33] The implication made by Verghese was that these five distortions serve to alienate the

Church from play. They are: a low view of the incarnation, based on the idea that flesh is sinful; the desire to flee from the world so as to escape its evils; man in abject dependence on God whose glory thereby diminishes man and makes him of little importance and worth; the emphasis on individual salvation at the expense of both our fellow human-beings and the rest of the creation; and finally, a low view of the sacraments and the way in which the finite can be used to mediate the infinite.

The first three of the above distortions result in a devaluing of human activities which by implication lowers the significance of play as well as denying the divine affirmation of the creation. This is the situation where play is seen as a children's activity and disproved of in low church pietism. The fourth distortion, that of an emphasis on individual salvation, devalues social interaction and, by implication, devalues the importance of play as a corporate activity. The fifth distortion, namely a low view of the sacraments, devalues symbolism, which is a vital element of play. Although the linking of these five areas with Augustine can be disputed, what is important is the fact that they are attitudes which are present within the Christian Church and which mitigate against play and devalue its significance. Once again, pietism does not fare well in our analysis. Whilst we are correct to realise that we are not divine, we should also recall that we are made in the divine image. If this image has become marred, then we should remember the words of Athanasius concerning Christ. 'He became human that we might become divine.'[34] The suggestion is that we need a richness and diversity in our Church life and worship if we are to be truly able to play and pray.

The question which has so far been left unanswered, is whether play is part of the image of God in which humanity has been created. To put it more succinctly, does God play? As was hinted at the end of chapter six, the answer to this question is coming to be seen as yes. The play of the Divine occurs in creative activity: creation in the beginning, creation within time and creation at the end of time.

The Jewish wisdom literature points towards the idea of divine play, with its vision of Wisdom sporting on the earth and taking delight in humanity. The word which is used for the action of Wisdom in Proverbs Ch.8.30f, is the same word which is translated as 'dance' in II Samuel, Chapter six, verses 5 and 21.[35] The model of God as dancer which we explored in chapter six implicitly includes the idea of God at play in His creative activity. The Greek fathers of the Church also saw creation as a form of play, noting that creation occurred freely and spontaneously, not as a result of the laws of necessity. God delights in His creation. Although creation is undoubtedly a serious business, being both meaningful and non-arbitrary, it also has about it a spontaneity and joy. These characteristics are all factors which we associate with play. True play always contains within itself the possibility of the new.

Moltmann notes the sadness associated with the child's question as to why God created the World. Although this question may be spontaneous in the mind of the child, Moltmann believes that it usually has its roots in the idea that all action must be useful.[36] We have to move beyond the idea that creation was necessary (albeit retaining the idea that it is not random or arbitrary), because this notion denies the freedom of God.

These ideas should not be taken to imply that God's creative action is capricious, for everything which he does is grounded in His good-will, His ευδοκια (eudokia). Creation is a part of God's deepest nature and, in as much as we can apply the terminology, God derives pleasure from creating. Creation, like play, is an activity which is meaningful but not necessary.[37] Work which is creative and pleasurable is therefore play, just as we hinted in section one of the present chapter. This is the point which was made so powerfully by Vanstone in his description of the garden made by two boys in his parish.[38] Their creative activity was absorbing and demanding but totally free and pleasurable; it would have to be described as play rather than as work.

Moltmann has developed his thought in this field since the early 1970s.[39] He now makes the important point that the Kingdom of God belongs to little children because only they know how to play. Everybody else has forgotten. We need to rediscover the ability to play and thereby to solve the unresolved contingencies of life.

Empty pews in Churches point to the wider impact and

occurrence of the loss of the ability to play (in the way in which it is being defined here), and the lack of spontaneity within the population.[40] There is always the question of 'Why go to Church?', and we are reminded of the fact that utility is high on the popular agenda. That part of the creation which is of no obvious use to the individual and the worship of the creator God are both classed as being of no use. The idea of worship as a free response to God is missing. As with so many other things in life, our response to God becomes a demand made upon us; an activity which has to compete for our time along with all the things which are useful or which need to be done. This is the reason why gimmicks are not the ultimate answer to church growth. They may draw people in, but they do not result in genuine play and worship and fail to generate a genuine response to God.[41] Once the church has attracted people, it needs to help them to learn how to worship freely and to play in the presence of God.

It is also important that we do not lose sight of the resurrection. Wesley Carr has linked the resurrection to the idea of play, noting that both move beyond the rational.[42] We should note that if creation is play, then the creative action which was involved in the resurrection must also be considered in this way.

What are the consequences of the above views for the Church? What are the Church's major unresolved contingencies; the questions which concern its whole existence and do not arise simply out of some local squabble? The answer may be similar to that which we all need to solve and which also concerns the population far beyond the church, namely that of the endtime. For each one of us, death looms ahead and we attempt to resolve the questions which this poses for us. We have hinted that play within the Church is one way in which this can occur. For the Church, it is the eschatological endtime which is of concern. The Pauline Church was well aware of this problem, expecting the eschaton to occur within the lifetime of its members, whereas today we postpone the discussion for a future time. If play is concerned with a preparation for future events, then the play of the Church in worship may be a means to resolve this tension. Through play, we can prepare to meet God face to face and to participate both in the heavenly banquet and in the celestial praise and worship of the Triune God.

Earlier in the present section, we noted a definition by the Hanson brothers which described the Church as: 'The Church is the People of God and it is called to be the Body of Christ.' If we accept this definition, then although we might anticipate the movement from the one to the other through our worship, it is only when we join in God's universal eschatological play that this transformation occurs in its entirety. At its best, the worship of the Church is proleptic of the time when this transformation will be complete.

When we used the criteria of play to consider the models of Dulles, each model had points in its favour as well as problems, although the numbers of points varied from model to model. The two models which filled the criteria of play the most closely were those of The Church as Mystical Communion and The Church as Sacrament. If we compare these models to the definition of the Hanson brothers, we then note that Dulles described the former model as encompassing both The People of God and The Body of Christ. However, Dulles' picture of The People of God was different to that of the Hansons and his closest match to their ideas on this point seems to be that of the Church as Sacrament. If we identify the Hansons' definition with a model in which The Church as Sacrament moves towards and becomes The Church as Mystical Communion, then this can indicate how the Hanson's description relates to the concept of the Church at Play. There is the implication that the church needs to focus itself on these models if it is to relate to the present age, complete with its various problems and to enable people to grow into true worship. This may have implications for the ways in which the church trains its members, especially its clergy, and the ways in which it prepares its forms of public worship.

We can see that the play of the Church is not only about the present time but has to point to the future. In identifying the reasons why people play, Kahn included recapitulation, in which unresolved problems are explored by imitation and anticipation, in which future activities are practised.[43] Both recapitulation and anticipation are powerful ideas within Christian worship and theology. In our worship we recapitulate the saving action of God in human history, centred in the life, death and resurrection of Jesus Christ. In worship we also anticipate the eschaton and our own resurrection. We look forward to the time when the creation no longer groans in travail (Romans Ch.8) but when, enjoying the perfect play of the kingdom, we meet God face to face. Although, at first sight, the above discussion about play may appear to say little about environmental crisis, the point is that a rediscovery of true play would be accompanied by a fundamental change of outlook towards the world. The present contention is that such an outlook which sees play as important is far closer to the pattern of The God who described Creation as good. It is therefore time for us to examine in more detail the ways in which worship can be understood as play and also to consider the ways in which this discussion can inform our understanding of liturgical practice.

Notes

1. This premise is interesting, because it implies that whereas at certain times in the past it was Christianity and the adoption of Christian practices which was believed to lead to a higher standard of living, albeit that the benefits were largely deferred until after death, this is no longer the case. This religious world-view of benefits beyond the grave has been rejected and popular belief has moved on. At present this appears to include the belief that it is possible to continually improve our lifestyle and perfect ourselves in the present world if we conform to a certain lifestyle which works in that world. From the Christian viewpoint this philosophy of life and economic growth contains a subtle form of pelagianism in which humanity is thought to be capable of perfecting itself without outside help.
2. Von Rad (1972) pp.61ff.
3. Moltmann (1985) pp.276–296.
4. Vanstone (1982).
5. Rayner p.99.
6. Moltmann (1973) pp.32f.
7. Jenkins, writing in his introduction to Moltmann (1973) pp.20f. We should note that this 'leisure culture' is not a universal phenomenon. In certain service professions, such as General Medical Practice, the work–load and expectations have increased dramatically. As a result, leisure time has been reduced to the point where it can be almost non-

existent unless a specific effort is made to produce the opportunity for such activities.

8. Jenkins, ibid.

9. Kahn p.22. It is instructive to observe that the variety of human approaches to sexual-intercourse, which is an important adult form of play, also fit these different categories.

10. Kahn p.120.

11. Cox p.24.

12. Moltmann (1973) p.26.

13. Moltmann (1973) pp.27ff.

14. Jenkins, writing in his introduction to Moltmann (1973), p.8.

15. Jenkins makes a similar point in his introduction to Moltmann (1973), although he expresses it a little differently. Freud also missed the point that most transition objects are grounded in a real object, but that the object has taken on a distorted significance. To see God as a transition object is not to see Him as a figment of our imagination but rather as a reality which has been distorted by the human mind and understanding.

16. This can be a very misleading statistic. It is quite possible for a congregation to decline in terms of the weekly attendance, yet increase in terms of the number of different people who worship each month or in terms of the commitment of that regular congregation.

17. Note the full form of this statement which is often and erroneously abbreviated to 'justification by faith'.

18. See also Tillich's other work, 'The Courage to Be', especially chapter six.

19. It could be argued that Tillich himself made a significant contribution to this circumscription of religion by rationality. Although there is some truth in this criticism, it misses both his insistence on Belief-ful Realism (see below) and his love of German poetic literature such as that of Goethe and Rilke. It also misses the point that all of his books are short in comparison to those of many other major theologians of his day.

20. Κοινονια is the Greek word used by the early church to describe the internal relationship between its members. Its direct translation into English is 'community' or 'fellowship', but the Greek also carries a greater sense of caring and unity in diversity than these English words do today.

21. McFadyen pp.16–18.

22. Winnicott's list of reasons for play are contained in his article 'Why Children Play', which can be found in Winnicott (1964).

23. Kahn (1971).

24. Kahn pp.120f.

25. First published in 1942, this article can be found in Winnicott (1964)

pp.149ff. Kahn has produced a separate list which differs from that of Winnicott in several ways (Kahn, pp.121–123).

26. Hanson and Hanson p.43.
27. These models are described in chapters two to six of Dulles.
28. Kierkegaard p.322.
29. H.Rahner p.65.
30. Cox pp.146ff.
31. Guiver pp.32f.
32. Oppenheimer (1965) pp.55f.
33. See Moltmann (1973).
34. Athanasius *De Incarnatione Verbi Dei, 54.*
35. Cox p.151.
36. Moltmann (1973) pp.39ff.
37. Moltmann (1973) pp.40ff.
38. Vanstone (1977) pp.30ff.
39. See Moltmann (1985). Of particular relevance are pp.310ff.
40. Oppenheimer (1965) p.58. This, of course, assumes that the seating capacity of the Church does not exceed the potential size of the congregation as is certainly the case with many rural buildings.
41. Oppenheimer (1965) p.60.
42. Carr pp.194ff.
43. Kahn pp.121–123.

Chapter 8

The Relevance of Worship

In chapter seven we began to consider the relationship between Christian worship and play. If this is a valid relationship then the understanding of play which we examined in section 7.3 should be able to inform our understanding of worship. It also serves to remind us that worship is not only about the present time but, like play, also reaches into the future. Indeed, it is worship above all else which informs and inspires the life of the Church. If the response of the Church to environmental crisis is to include a change of attitude then worship is important in bringing this change to fruition.

8.1 Worship as Play

In his book 'The Church in the Midst of Creation', Vincent Donovan begins by contrasting what he sees as traditional Roman Catholic and Protestant religious practices. He makes the point that whereas Catholic practice involved all of the bodily senses of sight, smell, taste, feeling and hearing (to which we might want to add a sense of the numinous, the holy), Protestant religion was centred heavily and centrally on the Word and therefore had a much less holistic approach to the creation. Catholic practice was sacramental in a way that Protestant practice could not be because Catholic practice was aware of the presence of the Holy in what appeared to be commonplace. Yet despite this approach, the Catholic tradition failed to speak out against the injustices of the world (including environmental damage) and to exercise that prophetic voice which should be part of the relationship between the Church and the World.[1] Donovan's claim that worship needs to draw on and relate to the whole of our lives and God's creation and not simply to our sense of hearing is surely correct, as is his implication that this needs to find expression in the cutting voice of prophecy. If we are serious when we state that we value the whole of the creation, then this creation should be reflected in the ways in which we worship.

There are a number of strong similarities between Tillich's account of the ways in which religious practice needed to be renewed (see section 7.2) and Donovan's overall premise for the renewal of the Church and its Worship. These ideas need to be related to the nature and the identity of the worshipping community. Although it is possible to worship God when we are alone and it is right that we should do so, the present focus is on the Church as a body and on communal rather than on individual worship. We are considering the people of God as they meet together and the attitudes and assumptions which they bring with them.

The obvious question to ask of these people as they meet together for worship, is that of what they do. This reflects the activist approach to life in which the individual asks 'What shall I do today?' However, this is not the right question for a worshipping community. For a people who meet before the God whom they worship as Father, Son and Holy Spirit, the correct question is rather that of who or what they are.[2] James Torrance has noted that if we go to church to participate in activities and thereby to please God, then this is a form of Pelagianism. For Torrance, our worship – in whatever form it may take – is the gift of participation in the communion of the Holy Trinity. This worship is worship through the Spirit and is centred in Christ. John Thompson is certainly correct when he notes that God does not accept us because of our worthy worship or because of what we do, but rather because of what Jesus Christ has done for us.

This view of worship relates well to the models of the Church which we examined in section 7.4. There we identified the 'Church as Sacrament' moving towards the 'Church as Mystical Communion'. Both of these models focus on what the people of God are and describe this in terms of sharing and participation with God. It is notable that both Torrance and Thompson, working within the Reformed tradition, have pointed towards the importance of the service of Holy Communion. Here, we recall in detail what it is that Christ has done for us, we acknowledge what we are and we state that we share in the body and blood of Christ.

Too often, worship has been seen as a private affair which is separate from the world which surrounds it. The Russian Orthodox theologian Alexander Schmemman has taken the opposite view and noted that it is important that we do not separate the private and the public in this way. Worship takes that which may start as private, but makes it into something which is essentially public and corporate. True worship is a function of the Church and not vice versa; it is one facet of the Church fulfilling itself as the Body of Christ, a source of spiritual nourishment for that Body. Worship should be an action of the Church in the World and not an escape from that world.[3]

This communal nature of worship is also reflected in the prayers which we use. The Lord's Prayer is written as a communal prayer, even when the prayer is said alone. We pray to 'Our Father', and ask for 'our daily bread'. It is 'our' sins which need forgiveness and 'we' who forgive the sins of others. We also ask God not to lead 'us' into temptation and to deliver 'us' from evil. There is no room for an individualistic approach to faith or to Christianity in this central prayer. This is not to argue that there may not be times when we wish to be alone to worship, or even to sit in isolation in a large congregation, for such worship will sometimes be appropriate. The point is, that we should always realise that we are part of a larger worshipping and praying community and that we have responsibilities towards this community.

If worship is communal rather than individualistic, then the question arises as to what type of communal activity it might be. Are there parallels which we can draw with other communal activities which will then illustrate our worship? If the true locus of play for the Church lies in its worship, is it also true that all our worship should bear the hallmarks of play, where play is as described above and remembering that this play is not trivial.

In his book 'The Spirit of the Liturgy', the Roman Catholic

liturgist Romano Guardini expressed this same idea in a chapter entitled 'The Playfulness of the Liturgy'. Geoffrey Wainwright is quick to observe that this activity is serious play, like that of children. Worship is rest on a working day and labour on a day of rest.[4] The problems with this approach are that in Hebrew the word '*abad* (the verb 'to serve') is used to indicate both work and worship and that the root of the word 'liturgy' is εργο (ergo), the Greek word for work. Moreover, the early church fathers saw prayer as κεποσ (kepos – hard work) and the monastic tradition adopted the phrase from Ecclesiasticus Ch.38 v34, 'laborare est orare' ('to work is to praise'). How can we resolve this apparent conflict between the descriptions of worship as both play and work?

The conclusion to reach is that there is no contradiction between defining worship and prayer in terms of work and understanding worship as the Church at play. In their origins, the above statements reflected a very different idea of work to that which we hold today. Work used to be a way of life rather than the alternative to leisure activities. It was only the emergence of organized labour at the time of the industrial revolution which brought the distinction between work and play into widespread use.[5] The play to which we are referring here is not the opposite of work – that role is fulfilled by leisure. The genuine play which is referred to here is a serious business and must be distinguished from leisure activities.

If worship is the Church at play, then the rules to the ordering of that play are provided by the liturgy. This implies that we can apply the rules and characteristics of play, as summarised in section 7.3, to Church worship. In some cases the links between these rules or characteristics and Church worship are trivial, and here the obvious similarity lends support to the theory that worship is play. However, other comparisons are more involved and throw interesting light on the internal workings of the Church, both nationally and locally.

If we consider first the rules of play and compare them to liturgy, then we should note that when people play, the rules serve to remove uncertainty and allow a full participation in the action. This is also true of liturgical structures. C.S. Lewis noted that just as 'whilst we still count the steps we do not dance', so the perfect liturgy is that of which we are unaware through familiarity.[6] Moreover, liturgical rules start from a given basis and then gradually change and emerge with time, as do the rules of play. In both liturgy and play the rules are complex and their organization and preparation can take considerably longer than the play or worship itself. These three comparisons serve to show the similarity between the rules of play and those of the liturgy. The fact that rules in play cannot be imposed on the players from outside is parallelled by the fact that liturgical revision is never universally accepted, especially by those people who were not involved in producing the changes.

A further example is provided by the statement that the rules of games are not inviolate and are broken to test the reaction of the other players. The same is true of liturgy, and the breaking of a rule without a sanction being applied may lead to a change of that rule for the group which is involved. By this mechanism different liturgies can evolve for different churches and the use of illegal liturgies can lead to a variety of results. As an example, the lack of applied sanctions against the use of the Roman Catholic Rite for Holy Communion in some Anglican churches has led to it becoming the norm for them, whereas the excommunication of Roman Catholic Bishops who continued to use the Tridentine Mass is typical of the schism which occurs when different players want to play using different sets of rules.

The most significant observation which we can make concerning these rules, is that which matched the fifth and final observation about play. This is that a lack of novelty results in stagnation and sensory deprivation, whilst excess novelty results in confusion. The former position corresponds to the use of the same form of service without change for a lifetime or more and is exemplified by the Book of Common Prayer services of the Church of England. There is nothing wrong with these services and they should continue to be used, but their exclusive and unimaginative use is not beneficial to the Church. The latter position of excess novelty corresponds to the situation where change is rapid and continuous, especially if there is no overlap with what went before. A new liturgy every week or a new prayer-book every year cannot be recommended. These lessons which have still not been learnt completely and taken to heart by the Church are the same as those which can be deduced from play, especially the play of young children.

If we turn our attention to the characteristics of play, then we first note that enjoyment and free-will are typical characteristics of play and that they should also be associated with good worship. A person who attends a religious service through coercion is unlikely to worship, and attendance by free-will in the present day is unlikely unless there is some sense of enjoyment or fulfilment.

A second point concerns the deduction that, in play, too much too soon is detrimental to growth, but that too little at a later stage of development leads to deprivation. If this is true, then we must take seriously the call for variety in our styles of worship. The worship which may help a long-term committed member of a Church may not be helpful to a person who is new to such worship. The worship which feeds the newcomer may not feed the long-term worshipper, even though they might need to attend in order to make that worship possible.

More significantly, play often involves the participants in overcoming the world, through their coming to terms with future events and by removing the anxiety which might be induced by such events. In worship this same coming to terms with the future can be demonstrated in several ways. Salvation is one clear means by which this occurs, in that the God who is worshipped provides the necessary route to overcome evil and suffering. Religious worship reminds us of our pain and death but also provides the mechanism whereby we can come to terms with it. The proleptic element in worship can also express this concept, in that worship can be regarded as the natural time and place (the Sitz-im-Leben) to experience a foretaste of the Kingdom of God. The theology of the Eucharist has often treated its subject in this way.[7] If the Eucharist is a foretaste of the Kingdom of God, then such worship of God can be seen as preparatory activity for the meeting of God face to face.

The use of symbols in play is clearly parallelled in worship, where objects take on a significance beyond their everyday value. These symbols are recognisable to those who are involved in the worship or who are aware of the rules but may appear meaningless to those who observe from the outside. Like the child who is indignant when told that his two crossed sticks are not an aeroplane, so many Christians are indignant when the consecrated elements of the Eucharist are treated as ordinary bread and wine. This parallel extends to the way in which the significance of symbols in compulsive play is similar to that which can occur in worship. In both cases the compulsive player is obsessed with finding the one true meaning of the symbol (or sacrament) and cannot tolerate either ambiguity or those people who hold to a different interpretation. The vehemence of those who hold opposing positions on the nature of the elements in the Eucharist serves to illustrate this point, with extremists on either side disagreeing with each other in ways which can become heated and violent.

We have also noted how compulsive behaviour can result from a disrupted game or a situation where the rules are changed before those who have the greatest unresolved needs and anxieties have been satisfied. In worship the parallel to this emerges when changes either occur or are proposed in the liturgy. Of the two, the proposal of a change can be seen as the larger threat since there is a greater element of the unknown involved. The use of The Book of Common Prayer in The Church of England again provides a good example. Opponents of The Alternative Services voiced what appeared to be an obsessional opposition to the introduction of these services and the publication of The Alternative Service Book in 1980. This obsession has continued ever since. The same pattern can be seen in the Church of England and the Anglican Communion more widely concerning the ordination of women to the priesthood. This issue of ordination comes into our remit of worship and play because liturgical worship, notably the Eucharist, is the situation where the ordination of women to the Priesthood ·is most obvious.

Finally, but most importantly, we note that play is concerned with reality and with the reconciliation of the individual with what is real. The Christian parallel here is quite clear, because worship is also concerned with what is real. Worship is an affirmation of the reality of the Triune God – Father, Son and Holy Spirit – and of our commitment to Him. Lindbeck noted that whereas theology provides the grammar for religious doctrines, in worship we affirm what we actually believe.[8] It is when we fall down and worship God, that we are making our deepest commitment to His living reality and if we are committed to the living reality of the triune God, then we should also make a commitment to His creation. Christian worship and its liturgical setting should celebrate the creation-salvation of God, whether this occurs in the past, present or future and whether it concerns the creation of the material, of time or the salvation wrought in Jesus Christ.

8.2 Worship within Time

The belief that worship and liturgy are, in part, a celebration of God's creation and therefore a celebration of time, runs counter to the understanding of worship in the early Church presented by the Anglican Benedictine and Liturgist Dom Gregory Dix. According to Dix, the pagan nature of contemporary culture meant that the early Church kept life and liturgy apart.[9] In his opinion, Christian worship was world-renouncing until the time of the emperor Constantine (who ruled AD 306-337) and that for this reason there could be no liturgy which was rooted within time. This view led Dix himself and scholars such as Cullmann and Duchesne to deny the presence of public cycles of daily prayer in the early Church. For them, references to hours of prayer referred exclusively to private occasions and the only public worship was the Eucharist, the service of Holy Communion. In this important respect, they saw worship before the Council of Nicaea (AD 325) as being very different to that of the post-Constantinian period. This was exemplified by the Liturgy of the Hours, such as Morning Prayer and Evening Prayer, which they believed had its origins in the rise of monasticism in the second century and only became public during the post Nicene period in the fourth century.[10]

It is now widely acknowledged that Dix was mistaken and that the daily prayer of the so-called Cathedral Office[11] during the fourth century was continuous with that which had existed from the earliest days of the Christian Church and was not a derivative of monastic practice.[12] The early Church met for non-eucharistic forms of Morning Prayer and Evening Prayer before the Council of Nicaea and these meetings were not held in private. The confusion concerning the apparent privacy of these gatherings may well have arisen from the custom of dismissing the catechumens (those who were preparing for baptism) prior to the end of the service and the blessing. Where Dix was correct, was in seeing daily worship as eschatological, but eschatological worship and expectation can only occur from within that which is to come to an end, namely time. As we shall see below, through its presence within time, daily prayer serves to sanctify time rather than to dismiss it. Such sanctification is then in accordance with the idea that time, as part of the created order, is of itself intrinsically good.

It is therefore important to examine the development of this daily prayer during the first few centuries of the Church and to consider its significance in terms of the beliefs and attitudes of the time. What interests us here is not the intricacies of which offices emerged when and what liturgical material they contained, but the questions of why these offices were important and what they signified then and can still signify today. The key issue is that of how they related to the idea of continuous prayer offered up to God by His creation and thereby affirmed the relationship between that Creation and its creator.

It is widely accepted that Jews of the first century observed some cycle of daily prayer, such as the reciting of the *shema* (their confession of faith) between dawn and sunrise and after sunset. This was accompanied by elements of the *berekah*, the blessing of God. Although early Jewish Christians continued to attend temple and synagogue ceremonies until cAD 85, when stringent efforts were made to exclude them, it is likely that they also met separately as this would have been the only way in which they could share in the Eucharist and in their worship of Christ. The contemporary Anglican liturgist Paul Bradshaw sees three non-eucharistic offices in the early Church of the first century. These were the *latreia*, a service of psalms, hymns and prayers; a kerygmatic liturgy of the Word, which would have included scripture readings and a proclamation of the work of Christ; and a didactic liturgy of the Word, including continuous and orderly study of the scriptures[13].

This idea of continuous prayer is decidedly biblical. It occurred in the Old Testament and it was taken up strongly by those who wrote the letters now contained in the New Testament Canon. In I Thessalonians, Paul enjoins his readers to pray night and day (Ch.3.v10) as well as to pray constantly (Ch.5.v17) and he repeated this message of constant prayer to the Christians at Rome (Romans Ch.12.v12). Moving beyond the Bible, Clement of Rome supported the idea of fixed times of prayer, as expressed in the sixtieth chapter of his letter to the Corinthians. In addition, the *Didache*, a manual of morals and teaching from the early second century recommended three daily hours of prayer (*Didache 8*). This theme was then developed in detail by the Christian writers of the second, third and fourth centuries. Further details of these observances and their development can be found in the works by Guiver, Bradshaw, Martimort and Taft.

Eastern monasticism regarded the offices as second best to the ideal of continuous prayer, seeing prayer as the sole content and purpose of life. The daily tasks were to be regarded as a background action to prayer rather than as work in their own right to which prayers should be added. This is a further example of a holistic approach to work. However, it was not only the monks who were encouraged to observe the liturgy of the hours in this way. In the Cappadocian work 'De Virginitate', which has traditionally been ascribed to Athanasius, the author proposes that the third, sixth, ninth and twelfth hours as well as midnight formed a pattern which should be kept by the laity[14]. This marks the imposition of the monastic office onto those who used the Cathedral form.

It is clear that the observance of certain hours and times is a pragmatic outworking of the concept of continuous prayer. It is likely that the hours of prayer arose naturally within the worshipping community and that they were later rationalised, partially to support their existence and continued practice and partially to provide a focus for the prayer at each hour and as an aid to spirituality. Whatever the reasons, the celebration of the hours of light and darkness became seen in a distinctly Christological sense within the early Church. The passing of the day at evening reminds us of the earthly death of Christ, but the gift of light in the morning speaks of the resurrection.

This is a development in which the hours of prayer have moved beyond being merely those times at which people pray and have come to signify aspects of Christian life and the divine activity in creation.

The idea of the gift of the light is also reflected in the early development in which Christ is symbolised as light, notably in the Johannine writings.[15] This development then provided the reason or justification for the use of prayer facing towards the sun rising in the east, an action which symbolised Christ, the light shining in the darkness.[16] Bradshaw notes that this practice may well reflect lost memories of ancestral sun worship, an influence which he claims can be detected in Essene practices, where the Messiah was referred to as the Great Luminary.[17]

This idea of an eschatological link is not confined merely to one of the hours of prayer. The whole concept of continuous prayer is likely to have been eschatological in its origin, especially as presented in St. Paul's earliest and most eschatological work, namely his first letter to the Thessalonians. Similar ideas applied in the desert community at Qumran, where the East was understood as the direction from which the Messiah was expected to come. This eschatological expectation can also be linked with the Lord's Prayer, and its call for the coming of God's Kingdom. The Christian cycle of Prayer can be seen not as a reflection on the present world with its diurnal and annual cycles, but as a waiting and a watching for the parousia. It can remind us of creation, of the transient nature of the world and universe in which we now live and the greater glory of that which awaits us.

The liturgy of the hours exists, at least in part, in order to sanctify time. Unfortunately, although the daily office was originally simple in nature and marked the passing of this time, the increasing complexities which gradually occurred served to alienate the office from the laity[18]. As an example, if the psalter was used within this worship, then it was necessary either for it to be known by heart or for the worshipper to be both literate and to own expensive manuscript books. The lengths to which some monastic orders went with their pattern of worship, made their observances totally impractical for anyone who had not devoted their whole life to this particular cause.

Martimort notes that in the above process, the 'veritas horarum', the truth of the hours, was lost.[19] No longer did the prayers reflect the changing time of the day and in this way sanctify time. Instead, the times of the services were altered in order to fit in with other matters of daily life, and the offices had to be said at a later time if they were omitted at their appointed hour. In this way prayer became deontological, being done for its own sake rather than for its true purpose, and in this way it lost the spontaneity which is the response of our inner being. When the synod of Cloveshoe, held in the year 747, required all English clergy to say seven offices in Church each day, it was assumed that members of the laity would also be present. What had begun as the monastic pattern of seven offices and a celebration of time in expectation of the parousia, was now being imposed on all. The twofold pattern of public worship in the Cathedral Office was lost, reflecting the idea that monasticism was a more perfect form of Christianity than the secular life.

By the thirteenth and fourteenth centuries the English laity had abandoned the daily offices of prayer and it was only Cranmer and then the Elizabethan Settlement which put any emphasis back onto daily services of Morning and Evening Prayer in the English Church. These services emerged during 1538-49 as simplifications of the traditional sevenfold pattern, with Morning Prayer containing elements of the traditional offices of mattins, lauds and prime, whilst Evensong contained elements of vespers and compline. Cranmer's work was inspired by the parallel work of Francisco De Quinones on the continent, with both Cranmer and Quinones recovering the traditional pattern of the Cathedral Office. Even so, we need to recognise that one reason for the production of Cranmer's public services was the refusal of congregations, who were used to pre-reformation ways, to receive communion on a regular weekly basis. By the eighteenth century many Churches had no regular services apart from that on a Sunday[20]. Despite the revival in England inspired by the Oxford Movement and the shortening of the weekday offices in the Act of Uniformity Amendment Act of 1872, the situation has again declined.

However, this approach is again legalistic, whereas the present need is to recover the original intention of the offices, which was that of continuous prayer in eschatological expectation; sanctifying time and marking its passage. What is required is a genuine reflection that we live within time, and that this is a time which moves onwards and yet which is sanctified and affirmed by the God whom we worship. Furthermore, the sanctification of time can be seen as the confirmation that God sanctifies the whole of His Creation. As Martimort notes, we need to rise above personal taste and make the prayer of the Church into our own prayer, meditating on the role of God in Salvation History, both past and present. A salvation which extends to the whole of creation and not just to a particular chosen people. We need to meditate on what is, rather than to continually strive after novelty[21]. It should then be possible for the Liturgy to become personalistic, with the capacity to change people's lives from within the faith[22]. If time and life are sanctified in the offices, then this should affect the way in which we live our daily lives and the way in which we relate to the rest of creation.

It is important to realise that this pattern of prayer rests both upon faith and upon a knowledge of God, both individually and in community. The liturgy of the hours involves an element of anamnesis, the recollection of the historical works of God. It is therefore prayer for the faithful. It may appear strange to us that the daily prayer of the early church did not include teaching or, in many cases, even readings from the scriptures. Yet within the community of the faithful these elements were not strictly necessary on every occasion. We need to distinguish between the offices for the faithful, with their elements of anamnesis and sanctification, and the very different role of kerygma, with its direction to those who are outside the Christian body. The early church appears to have known this distinction, a distinction which today we have largely forgotten.

Services which may well meet the needs of a particular congregation, may be of no use in drawing new members into that body. In a similar way, services which are designed to appeal to those people who do not normally attend public worship will quite naturally not provide for the needs and desires of the committed Christian. Both of these patterns are important, not only for their balance between outreach and support of the faithful, but because of what they say about the attitude of the Church to the World. A service for the faithful may take us into a deep appreciation of God's love towards us but it can fail to remind us or make us a part of the fact that God's love extends to all that He has made, to the whole of His Creation. This failure can be rectified by services which try to reach beyond the regular worshippers, albeit that these services may fail to evoke a depth of response and fail to sanctify creation and time.

This sanctification of time can be linked to the Eucharist, for the Eucharist stands both outside time and within it. It is an anamnesis of the action of Christ and a prolepsis of the Kingdom of God. The liturgy of the Hours takes this impingement of the Eucharist onto time both into time and throughout time.[23] In a similar way, the daily offices can be seen as a prolongation of the Eucharist on the level of daily life. As in the monastic ideal, it may then be possible for time to become known only as a time for prayer, but with the acts of living themselves forming the prayer through their being sanctified rather than them being merely a backdrop. The whole of our lives become outworkings of our prayer and our actions in the world should reflect our worship of the God who is the creator of all.

If the whole of time can become a time for prayer in this way, then this not only recovers the sense of continual prayer which we examined above, but can also make real the early ideal of eschatological expectancy. If this is the case, then we not only wait for the parousia, but also act proleptically as we view the world through the eyes of Christ in the power of His continual presence. We are called on to treat the creation around us in a way which is a foretaste of the Kingdom of God.

8.3 Worship beyond Time

When he linked the Eucharist to time through the saying of the daily offices, Alexander Schmemman regarded the Eucharist in an eschatological sense, looking forward to the end of time.[24] Although the events which are actualised within the Eucharist are past events from our perspective (Jesus Christ died and rose during the first century), from the eschatological perspective they are events which are outside time. For this reason they are truly eternal (as distinct from sempiternal, a term for those things which exist at all moments within time). Although the Messiah came once within History, because He is God He is outside time and also comes in His Kingdom at the gathering together of the Church at the parousia (the coming of Christ in judgement). In this sense, the Eucharist can be seen as proleptic of the parousia, making it present now and enabling the Church to be a prolepsis or foretaste of the Kingdom of God. If the eschaton marks the gathering of the whole creation together with God and not merely the gathering together of the human race, then the Eucharist must relate to the whole of the creation.[25]

This discussion can appear to be dualistic and world-renouncing, but this is not the case. The coming of the eternal within time both affirms and sanctifies time, especially if we can see the prayer of the hours as taking the Eucharist into time and throughout time. Rather than being emptied, time is then fulfilled. Taft sees the Eucharistic liturgy as the Sitz-im-Leben of Christ's saving action – not simply a memory, but a way in which we become that which we celebrate.[26] The theme of worship is again linked to being. Sanctification enters into the temporal and time is eschatological both proleptically and in the future.

Shortly after Alexander Schmemman wrote about these ideas, Moltmann produced his 'Theology of Hope' and Pannenberg developed his idea of 'Revelation as History.'[27] Both of these regard the eschaton as transformation and consider its proleptic anticipation. It is important to remember that we can only understand the Eucharist in this way, as prolepsis and anamnesis (as both a foretaste and a remembrance), because time moves forward and is not cyclical. In technical terms, time is a single-valued function. We celebrate the fact that God touches us now in a real decisive encounter and not as a repetition of exactly the same encounter as has gone before. We are moving through time towards the divine fulfilment. This is why Taft can see the Eucharist as having its own special time, the kairos, which is outside the daily liturgical cycle. Eucharistic time is not cyclical, for it is both within time and outside time.[28] It does not recur every week or every year in the same way, for not only has the year moved on, but the Eucharist also draws that which is eternal into time. This idea of special time is the reason why Sunday can be justified as the primary eucharistic time, for Sunday is the time of resurrection. Sunday is the place within time when the decay which is concomitant with time is conquered and time is thereby transcended. Sunday is the day when, in the Eucharist, we give thanks for God's re-creation. This re-creation includes the salvation wrought on the cross.

This eucharistic view of Sunday has to be contrasted with the Jewish Sabbath, the day of rest, the day in which is the commemoration of the creation in all of its fulness and goodness. The Christian Sunday is the eighth day, the day after the Sabbath, the time of God's new action. It is a day beyond the created order, the day of messianic fulfilment within time. Christ rested in death on the Sabbath day, and rose on the eighth day – the first day of the new creation when we experience the first-fruits of the Holy Spirit.

The Eucharist is related to time, but what of its application to life and to space, to the whole of the creation? Whilst we should never forget the saving action of Christ on the cross and the resurrection, we should not be blind to the fact that these are a part of God's overall creative action. We must continue to understand the Eucharist in terms of salvation and forgiveness of sins, but to these elements we must add its celebration of the whole creation. Both of these understandings shed light on the questions of suffering and finitude, questions which apply both to humanity and to the environment which we have placed under threat. It is sometimes claimed that recent trends in eucharistic liturgy have glorified the creation and diminished the work of Christ. This criticism can be answered if we ensure that our liturgy both states the divine origins of the creation and acknowledges that it is also in need of salvation. We should never give the impression that all is well within the garden.

It is therefore entirely appropriate that in the service of Holy Communion our understanding of the Eucharistic prayer is moving away from a position which sees one particular

moment as the point of consecration and rather sees the consecration as occurring within the context of the prayer as a
whole. Consecration of the bread and wine is only possible in
the context of the whole service and not by the use of a magic
formula. This is illustrated well in the Church of England by
contrasting the instructions for the consecration of additional
bread and/or wine in the Book of Common Prayer and in The
Alternative Service Book 1980. In the former a formula is
recited, whereas in the later it is requested that the additional
bread and/or wine be part of the same bread and wine which
have already been consecrated and consumed. The former
gives the impression of a remote God who impinges on time at
one moment and in one place, whereas the latter recognises
that God continually indwells His creation.

The Eucharist is only the Eucharist because we gather
together in Christ's name; because we share the Word of God;
because we break bread together; because we believe that the
risen Christ is always with us. However, we can also go further
than this, because if the whole world is redeemed through
Christ, then it is the whole world which is offered up: a giving
back to God of that which is His. The Eucharist then becomes
a thanksgiving which embraces the whole of creation.

There are a number of consequences of this understanding
which are important in our present context. The first is that if
the whole of the creation is to be redeemed, or is in the
process of being redeemed, and yet we fail to reflect this in the
Eucharist and fail to reflect the love of God for His created
world, then what does this say about the meaning of our so-
called eucharistic services? Is it possible that we can only have
a valid Eucharist (that is, that we can only truly give thanks),
if we truly care for the world about us and give thanks for it
too? A further consequence is that if we ignore the needs of
the hungry people of the world, then the bread which we share
in the communion service becomes an empty symbol.

In opening our eucharistic worship to the wider world in the
above ways, we are not falling prey to nature worship but are
following the tradition which sees God as immanent as well as
transcendent. The body and blood of Christ, as found in the
bread and the wine, speak to us and can make present for us
God's sacrificial love for that which He has made. The Holy

Spirit dwells in creation and the Eucharist can speak of our care for that creation. If we fail in this particular aspect of eucharistic ministry and fail to care and give thanks for the work of God, then our services will be empty shells. If we fail to understand our role as stewards in the world, then how can we truly give thanks?

This is not to suggest that we should adopt a pelagian view of salvation, and come to believe that the Eucharist is justified by our works, for in both cases we are dependent solely upon the grace of God. It rather says something about the whole of our approach to life and that the Eucharist is a part of that whole approach and not an extra to be added on. Both in the ways in which it relates to our understanding of time and in its relationship with the creation, the Eucharist can be a valid Christian response to the world and to our place within that world. It is an example of the way in which traditional Christian practice and theological thought can take account of ecological issues and be sensitive to the needs of the present world. However, it can only be these things if we truly consider what it is that we are doing and why we are doing them rather than going through the motions because that is what we are supposed to do.

The very heart of Christian worship actually says something not only about our own relationship with God, but also about the relationships of both God and ourselves with the whole of the creation. This worship needs to move from being merely our worship when we meet in Church until it becomes that state in which it is the worship of God throughout the whole of our lives. The distinctive Christian response to a threatened creation is the Eucharist. A rediscovered Eucharist which permeates the whole of life and which challenges us to be prophetic as we take it with us into all that we do in the world. A Eucharist which leads us to continually affirm and explore the relationship which exists between Christ and the whole of the creation.

Ultimately, the Christian response has to do with Jesus Christ – it can do no other and still remain Christian. If the Christian faith teaches Jesus as the Incarnate Son of God, then to do otherwise is to deny that there is any point to the Christian faith at all. However, this response cannot be imposed on people without listening to what they are saying to us. It has to be presented as a real response to the real questions which are posed by the world of the present day: Questions which are posed both by the world around us and by our attitude towards that world and questions which matter to people at the deepest level. Only if the Christian faith can do this will it be seen as relevant by those who ask the questions.

Notes

1. Donovan pp1–5. Donovan's contrast of Catholic and Protestant practice is fairly narrow, in that it ignores both the cross-fertilization of the Oxford Movement and Anglo-Catholicism and also the contribution of the Orthodox Churches.
2. This idea has been presented and discussed by J.B. Torrance in his article 'The Vicarious Humanity of Christ', pp.127–147 of T.F. Torrance (1981). See also J. Thompson p.363.
3. Schmemman pp.21ff.
4. Wainwright p.27.
5. This is not to condone the fact that the majority of the population had no leisure time, but to observe that in the rural communities which existed, most people accepted their way of life without question. Something similar is seen in so-called primitive tribal cultures where the distinction between work and play is unknown – there is simply a way of life to be lived.
6. Lewis p.12. See also Guiver, p.33.
7. E.g. see Schmemman pp.57ff.
8. Lindbeck pp.73ff.
9. These opinions of Dix, presented in his important work 'The shape of the liturgy' (1945) have been discussed by Taft pp.331ff.
10. See Schmemman pp.40–43, who summarises both this and the opposing point of view as well as arguing the case for early public worship.
11. This nomenclature is derived from that of Baumstark, who used it to denote popular public ceremonial centred around the Bishop, as distinct from the Monastic Office which centred on meditation. See also Taft p.32.
12. This view does not receive universal consent, but has been powerfully argued by writers such as Taft.
13. Bradshaw (1978) pp1–2.
14. Bradshaw (1981) pp.102f.
15. See John Ch.1.vv4–9, Ch.8.v12, Ch.9.v5 and Ch.12.vv45–46; I John Ch.1.vv5–7 and Ch.2.vv8–11; Rev. Ch.21.vv22–26.

16. These ideas can also be seen in Clement of Alexandria's Stromateis, VII.7.43.
17. Bradshaw (1981) pp.10ff.
18. E.g. Martimort pp.180f.
19. See Martimort pp.176ff. This phrase was developed by the Second Vatican Council.
20. See Guiver pp.95ff. for an elaboration on some of these issues.
21. Martimort pp.273ff.
22. Taft pp.259ff.
23. Schmemman pp.33ff.
24. Schmemman ibid.
25. From this perspective, the words for the preparation of the gifts, which are said after the offertory procession in the Roman Rite and are optional in some Anglican liturgies, are a helpful part of the celebration. One form of these words is: 'Blessed are you Lord, God of all Creation. Through your goodness we have this bread to offer, which earth has given and human hands have made. It will become for us the bread of life', and 'Blessed are you Lord, God of all Creation. Through your goodness we have this wine to offer, fruit of the vine and work of human hands. It will become our spiritual drink.'
26. See Taft for a discussion of this idea.
27. Moltmann 1967; Pannenberg 1968a.
28. It is sometimes thought that the time in the daily office is cyclical. However, it would be more accurate to state that it is helical or spiral since when it moves round to the same time of the day (circular motion) time has also moved forward (linear motion).

Bibliography

Allison, C.F., *The Cruelty of Heresy. An Affirmation of Christian Orthodoxy*, SPCK, London, 1994.

Ambler, R., *Global Theology, The Meaning of Faith in the present World Crisis*, SCM, London, 1990.

Arguile, R., 'A Green Theology?', *New Blackfriars*, 72, pp.517-525, 1991.

Athanasius, 'Contra Gentes' and 'De Incarnatione', edited and translated by R.W. Thomson. Oxford Early Christian Texts, OUP, Oxford, 1971. or 'St. Athanasius on The Incarnation', Mowbray, London and Oxford, 1953.

Balasuriya, T., *Planetary Theology*, SCM, London, 1984.

Balthasar, H. Urs von, *Prayer*, American Edition, Ignatius Press, San Francisco, 1986.

Barbour, I.G., *Religion in an Age of Science*, SCM, London, 1990.

Barr J., *The Garden of Eden and The Hope of Immortality*, SCM, London, 1992.

Barrett, C.K., *The Gospel According to St. John*, Second Edition, SPCK, London, 1978.

Barth, K., *Church Dogmatics III, The Doctrine of Creation, Part One*, English Translation, T.&T. Clark, Edinburgh, 1958.

Barton, J., 'Theology and Other Sciences', *Theology*, 99, pp.52-58, 1996.

British Council of Churches, *The Forgotten Trinity*, London, 1989.

Baumstark, A., *Comparative Liturgy,* English Translation, Mowbray, London and Oxford 1958.

Bonhoeffer, D., *Letters and Papers from Prison*, Enlarged Edition, English Translation, SCM, London, 1971.

Bradley, I., *The Celtic Way*, Darton, Longman and Todd, London, 1993.

Bradshaw, P.F., *The Origins of the Daily Office*, Alcuin, London, 1978.

Bradshaw, P.F., *Daily Prayer in the Early Church*, Alcuin Collection 63, SPCK, London, 1981.

Brown, D., *The Divine Trinity*, Duckworth, London, 1985.

Brunner, E., *Dogmatics II, The Christian Doctrine of Creation and Redemption*, English Translation, Lutterworth, London, 1952.

Buckley-Golder, D.H., *Acid Deposition*, ETSU Report R.23, Department of Energy, London, 1984.

Bultmann, R., *The Gospel of John, A Commentary*, English Translation, Basil Blackwell, Oxford, 1971.

Calvert, W.M., *God to Enfold Me*, Grail, (dist. Gracewing/Fowler Wright, Leominster, England), 1993.

Carr, W., *The Pastor as Theologian*, SPCK, London, 1989.

Cowling, E.B., 'Acid Deposition in Historical Perspective', *Environmental Science and Technology*, *16*, pp.110A-123A, 1982.

Cox, H., *The Feast of Fools*, Harvard University Press, 1969.

Cross, F.L. and Livingstone, E.A. (eds), *The Oxford Dictionary of the Christian Church*, Second Revised Edition, OUP, Oxford, 1983.

Cupitt, D., *Taking Leave of God*, SCM, London, 1980.

Daly, G., *Transcendence and Immanence, A Study in Catholic Modernism and Integralism*, OUP, Oxford, 1980.

Daly, G., *Creation and Redemption*, Gill and Macmillan, Dublin, 1988.

Davies, P., *God and the New Physics*, Pelican, London, 1984.

Day, J., *God's Conflict with the Dragon and the Sea*, CUP, Cambridge, 1984.

Deane-Drummond, C., 'God and Gaia: Myth or Reality?', *Theology*, *95*, pp.277-285, 1992.

Dickinson, R.E. and Cicerone, R.J., 'Future global warming from atmospheric trace gases', *Nature*, 319, pp.109-115, 1986.

Dillistone, F.W., *Christianity and Symbolism*, Collins, London, 1955. Reissued by SCM, London, 1985.

Dix, G., *The Shape of the Liturgy*, 2nd Edition, Dacre Press, 1945.

DoE (Department of the Environment), *Ozone in the United Kingdom*, First Report of the United Kingdom Photochemical Oxidants Review Group, London, 1987a.

DoE (Department of the Environment), *Stratospheric Ozone*, Report of the United Kingdom Stratospheric Ozone Review Group, London, 1987b.

Donovan, V.J., *The Church in the Midst of Creation*, Orbis, Maryknoll, 1989; SCM, London, 1992.

Dostoyevsky, F., *The Brothers Karamazov*, Penguin, London 1958.

Dulles, A., *Models of The Church (2nd Ed.)*, Gill and Macmillan, Dublin, 1988.

Dunn, J.D.G., *Romans 1-8; Word Biblical Commentary 38A*, Word Books, Dallas, 1988.

Evans, C.F., *Saint Luke*, SCM/TPI, London/Philadelphia 1990.

Feuerbach, L., *The Essence of Christianity*, 1841. English language editions include that published by Harper and Row, New York, 1957.

Ford, D.F., (ed.) *The Modern Theologians*, Basil Blackwell, Oxford, 1989.

Fox, M., *Original Blessing*, Bear and Co., Santa Fe, 1983.

Fynn, *Mr God This is Anna*, Collins, London, 1974.

Garrison, J., *The Darkness of God: Theology after Hiroshima*, SCM, London, 1982.

Gill, R., *A Textbook of Christian Ethics*, T. & T. Clark, Edinburgh, 1985.

Guardini, R., *The Spirit of The Liturgy,* English Translation, Sheed and Ward, 1930.

Guiver, G., *Company of Voices – Daily Prayer and the People of God*, SPCK, London, 1988.

Gunton, C., *The Promise of Trinitarian Theology*, T.&T. Clark, Edinburgh, 1991.

Gutierrez, G., *A Theology of Liberation*, English Translation SCM, London, 1974.

Hanson, A.T. and Hanson, R.P.C., *The Identity of The Church*, SCM, London, 1987.

Hartshorne, C., *Philosophers Speak of God* (ed. with W.L. Reese), University of Chicago Press, 1953.

Hauerwas, S., *The Peaceable Kingdom: A Primer in Christian Ethics*, SCM, London, 1983.

Hawking, S.W., *A Brief History of Time*, Bantam and Transworld, London, 1988.

Hendry, G.S., *Theology of Nature*, Westminster Press, New York, 1980.

Hodgson, P.C. and King, R.H., *Christian Theology – An Introduction to its Tradition and Tasks*, SPCK, London, 1983.

Hough, A.M., 'Acid Deposition at Elevated Sites – A discussion of the processes involved and the Limits of Current Understanding', pp.1-47 of *Acid Deposition at High Elevation Sites*, ed. Unsworth, M.H. and Fowler, D., Kluwer Academic Publishers, Dordrecht, 1988.

Hough, A.M., 'The Development of a Two-Dimensional Global Tropospheric Model: The Model Chemistry', *Journal of Geophysical Research*, 96, pp7325-7362, 1991.

Hough, A.M. and Derwent, R.G., 'Computer Modelling Studies of the Distribution of Photochemical Ozone Production between different Hydrocarbons', *Atmospheric Environment*, 21, pp.2015-2033, 1987.

Hough, A.M. and Derwent, R.G., 'Changes in the Global Concentration of Tropospheric Ozone due to Human Activities', *Nature*, 344, pp.645-648, 1990.

Isaksen, I.S.A. and Hov, O., 'Calculation of trends in the tropospheric concentration of O_3, OH, CO, CH_4 and NO_x', *Tellus*, 39B, pp.271-285, 1987.

Jantzen, G.M., *God's World, God's Body*, Darton, Longman and Todd, London, 1984.

Jantzen, G.M., *Julian of Norwich*, SPCK, London, 1987.

Johnstone, W., *Exodus*, Sheffield Academic Press, 1990.

Kahn, J.H., *Human Growth and the Development of Personality*, 2nd edition, Pergammon, Oxford, 1971.

Kelly, J.N.D., *Early Christian Doctrines*, Fifth Edition, A.& C. Black, London, 1977.

Kierkegaard, *Christian Discourses*, English Translation, OUP, New York, 1961.

Kitamori, K., *The Theology of the Pain of God*, John Knox Press, Richmond, 1965.

Lewis, C.S., *Letters to Malcolm*, Collins, London, 1969.

Lindbeck, G., *The Nature of Doctrine: Religion and Theology in a Postliberal Age*, Westminster Press, Philadelphia, 1984.

Lovelock, J., *Gaia, A New Look at Life on Earth*, OUP, Oxford, 1979.

Lovelock, J., *The Ages of Gaia*, OUP, Oxford, 1988.

MacKenzie, I.M., *The Anachronism of Time*, Canterbury Press, Norwich, 1993.

Macquarrie, J., *Thinking about God*, SCM, London, 1975.

Macquarrie, J., *Principles of Christian Theology*, revised ed., SCM, London, 1977.

Macquarrie, J., *In Search of Deity: An Essay in Dialectical Theism*, SCM, London, 1984.

Macquarrie, J., *Jesus Christ in Modern Thought*, SCM/TPI, London/Philadelphia, 1990.

McDonagh, S., *To Care for the Earth. A Call to a New Theology*, Geoffrey Chapman, London, 1986.

McFadyen, A., *The Call to Personhood*, CUP, Cambridge, 1990.

McFadyen, A., 'The Trinity and Human Individuality: The Conditions for Relevance', *Theology*, 95, pp10-17, 1992.

McFague, S., *Models of God, Theology for an Ecological Nuclear Age*, SCM, London, 1987.

Martimort, A.G. (ed.), *The Church at Prayer IV – The Liturgy of Time*, Geoffrey Chapman, London, 1983.

Meredith, A.G., *The Cappadocians*, Geoffrey Chapman, London, 1995.

Moberly, W., 'Old Testament' and 'New Testament': The Propriety of the Terms for Christian Theology', *Theology*, 95, pp26-31, 1992.

Moltmann, J., *Theology of Hope*, English Translation, SCM, London, 1967.

Moltmann, J., *Theology and Joy*, English Translation, SCM, London, 1973.

Moltmann, J., *The Crucified God*, English Translation, SCM, London, 1974.

Moltmann, J., *The Future of Creation*, English Translation, SCM, London, 1979.

Moltmann, J., *The Trinity and the Kingdom of God*, English Translation, SCM, London, 1981.

Moltmann, J., *God in Creation. An Ecological Doctrine of Creation*, English Translation, SCM, London, 1985.

Moltmann, J., *The Way of Jesus Christ: Christianity in Messianic Dimensions*, English Translation, SCM, London, 1990.

Moltmann, J., *History and the Triune God*, English Translation, SCM, London, 1991.

Montefiore, H., (ed.) *Man and Nature*, Collins, London, 1975.

Nicholls, D., *Deity and Domination – Images of God and the State in the Nineteenth and Twentieth Centuries*, Routledge, London, 1988.

Noth, M., *A History of Pentateuchal Traditions*, English Edition, Scholars Press, Chico, California, 1981.

Oppenheimer, H., *The Character of Christian Morality*, Mowbray, Oxford, 1965.

Oppenheimer, H., 'Ourselves, Our Souls and Bodies', *Studies in Christian Ethics*, *4*, pp.1-21, 1991.

Pannenberg, W., 'Dogmatic Theses on the Doctrine of Revelation', in *Revelation as History*, (ed. W. Pannenberg), New York, 1968a.

Pannenberg, W., *Jesus – God and Man*, English Translation, SCM, London, 1968b.

Pannenberg, W., *Systematic Theology Volume 1*, English Translation, Eerdmans, Michigan/T.&T. Clark, Edinburgh, 1991.

Peacocke, A.R., *Creation and the World of Science*, OUP, Oxford, 1979.

Peacocke, A.R., *Theology for a Scientific Age*, Enlarged Edition, SCM, London, 1993.

Platten, S., 'Authority and Order in Creation', *Theology*, *94*, pp.22-30, 1991.

Polkinghorne, J., *The Way the World is*, Triangle-SPCK, London, 1983.

Polkinghorne, J., *Reason and Reality*, SPCK, London, 1991.

Rahner, H., *Man at Play*, Herder and Herder, New York, 1967.

Rahner, K., *Theological Investigations IV*, English Translation, Darton, Longman and Todd, London, 1966.

Rahner, K., *Theological Investigations XVI*, English Translation, Darton, Longman and Todd, London, 1979.

Ramanathan, V., Cicerone, R.J., Singh, H.B. and Kiehl, J.T., 'Trace gas trends and their potential role in climate change', *Journal of Geophysical Research*, *90*, pp.5547-5566, 1985.

Ramsey, I.T., 'Talking about God'. This essay has appeared in a number of publications, for instance p.202-223 in *Words about God*, I.T. Ramsey (ed.), SCM, London, 1971.

Rayner, E., *Human Development: An Introduction to the Psychodynamics of Growth, Maturity and Ageing* (3rd edition), Unwin Hyman, 1986.

Robinson, J.M. and Cobb, J.B. (eds), *Theology as History*, Harper and Row, New York, 1967.

Sarot, M., 'Suffering of Christ, Suffering of God?', *Theology*, *95*, pp.113-118, 1992.

Schmemman, A., *Introduction to Liturgical Theology*, English Edition, Faith Press, London, 1966.

Song, C.S., *Third-Eye Theology. Theology in Formation in Asian Settings*, English Edition, Lutterworth, Guildford, 1980.

Soskice, J.M., *Metaphor and Religious Language*, OUP, Oxford, 1985.

Soskice, J.M., 'Creation and Relation', *Theology*, *94*, pp.31-39, 1991.

Stevenson, J., *A New Eusebius*, revised edition by W.H.C. Frend, SPCK, London, 1987.

Stevenson, J., *Creeds, Councils and Controversies,* revised edition by W.H.C. Frend, SPCK, London, 1989.

Studdert-Kennedy, G.A., *The Hardest Part*, Hodder and Stoughton, London, 1918.

Taft, R.F., *The Liturgy of the Hours in East and West,* English Translation, The Liturgical Press, Collegeville, U.S.A., 1986.

Teilhard de Chardin, P., *The Phenomenon of Man*, English Translation, Collins, London, 1959.

Thompson, J., 'Modern Trinitarian Perspectives', *Scot. Journ. of Theol.*, *44*, pp.349-365, 1991.

Thompson, R., 'Immanence Unknown: Graham Ward and the Neo-Pagans', *Theology*, *95*, pp.18-26, 1992.

Tillich, P., *The Protestant Era*, Chicago University Press, 1948.

Tillich, P., *The Shaking of the Foundations*, SCM, London, 1949.

Tillich, P., *The Courage to Be*, Nisbet & Co., London or Fontana, London, 1962.

Tillich, P., *Systematic Theology I*, reissued by SCM, London, 1978a.

Tillich, P., *Systematic Theology II*, reissued by SCM, London, 1978b.

Tillich, P., *Systematic Theology III*, reissued by SCM, London, 1978c.

Torrance, T.F., (ed) *The Incarnation – Ecumenical Studies in the Nicene-Constantinopolitan Creed*, The Handsel Press, Edinburgh, 1981.

Torrance, T., *Space, Time and Resurrection*, OUP, Oxford, 1976.

Tyrrell, G., *Essays on Faith and Immortality*, London, 1914.

Vanstone, W.H., *Love's Endeavour Love's Expense. The Response of Being to the Love of God*, Darton, Longman and Todd, London, 1977.

Vanstone, W.H., *The Stature of Waiting*, Darton, Longman and Todd, London, 1982.

Volz, A., and Kley, D., 'Evaluation of the Montsouris series of ozone measurements made in the nineteenth century', *Nature*, *332*, pp.240-242, 1988.

Von Rad, G., *Genesis*, English Edition (revised), SCM, London, 1972.

Von Rad, G., *Old Testament Theology I*, English Edition, SCM, London, 1975.

Von Rad, G., *Old Testament Theology II*, English Edition, SCM, London, 1965.

Wainwright, A., *Doxology: The Praise of God in Worship, Doctrine and Life,* Epworth, London, 1980.

Weiser, A., *The Psalms*, English Edition, SCM, London, 1962.

Westerman, C., Isaiah 40-66, English Edition, SCM, London, 1969

Williams, R. D., 'God and Risk', pp.11-23 of *The Divine Risk*, ed. R. Holloway, Darton, Longman and Todd, London, 1990.

White, L., 'Historical roots of our ecological crisis', *Science*, *155*, pp.1203-7, 1967.

Whitehead, A.N., *Process and Reality: An Essay in Cosmology*, CUP, Cambridge 1929.

Wiles, M., *Working Papers in Doctrine*, SCM, London, 1976.

Winnicott, D., *The Child, The Family and The Outside World*, Pelican, London, 1964.

Wisdom, J., 'Gods', pp.9-168 of *Philosophy and Psychoanalysis*, Basil Blackwell, Oxford, 1953.

WMO (World Meteorological Organisation), *Atmospheric Ozone 1985, WMO Global Ozone Research and Monitoring Project, Report No. 16*, WMO. Geneva, 1986.

Wren, B., *What Language Shall I Borrow? God-Talk in Worship: A Male Response to Feminist Theology*, SCM, London, 1989.

Wright, N.T., *Who was Jesus?*, SPCK, London, 1992.

Young, N., *Creator, Creation and Faith*, Collins, London, 1976.

Zahrnt, H., *The Question of God*, SCM, London, 1971.

Zizioulas, J.D., *Being as Communion, Studies in Personhood and The Church*, Darton, Longman and Todd, London, 1985.

Name Index

Subject Index